Moving Mountains

Michele Michaels

Foreword by
Erin Thiele

RestoreMinistries.net

NarrowRoad Publishing House

Moving Mountains
Michele Michaels

Published by:
NarrowRoad Publishing House
POB 830
Ozark, MO 65721 U.S.A.

The materials from Restore Ministries were written for the sole purpose of encouraging women. For more information, visit us at:

EncouragingWomen.org
RestoreMinistries.net

Permission from the author has been given to those who wish to print or photocopy this book for themselves or others, strictly for encouragement and informational purposes; however, such copies or reprints cannot be sold in any form without prior written permission from the author.

Unless otherwise indicated, most Scripture verses are taken from the *New American Standard Bible* (NASB). Scripture quotations marked KJV are taken from the *King James Version* of the Bible, and Scripture quotations marked NIV are taken from the *New International Version*. Our ministry is not partial to any particular version of the Bible but **loves** them all so that we are able to help every woman in any denomination who needs encouragement and who has a desire to gain greater intimacy with her Savior.

Copyright © 2020 by Erin Thiele

Cover Design by Tara Thiele

ISBN: 1-931800-19-7
ISBN13: 978-1-931800-19-8
Library of Congress Control Number: 2020904178

Table of Contents

1. Moving Your Mountains 5
2. Owe No Man 13
3. Imagine 20
4. Promises 27
5. Baby Steps 40
6. Opposition 47
7. Simply Speak 61
8. Final Hurdle? 72
9. Feelings 83
10. Mountains to Climb 94
11. Tarry 103
12. Teetering on the Brink of Prosperity 110
13. A Purse with Holes 123
14. Eaten Alive 130
15. Rebuild the Temple 136
16. Giving Frenzy 142
17. You Owe Me Nothing 147
18. By Grace 156
19. Valley of Humiliation 162
20. My Jonathan 169
21. Mountain Moved 175
    Epilog 183
    About the Author 188

Foreword

It's been years since the Feminist Movement robbed women out of their rightful roles and blessings of how God designed women to be. Though it's goal was to give women the same rights as men, it has served to cause women to have no choice but to become single mothers, provide not only for themselves but often their male cohabitant. Women have not freed themselves from men, as it said it was set out to accomplish, but instead, women have become obsessed with having a man, any man at any cost. Not surprisingly the Bible's prophet said times like this would come. Isaiah 4:1 The Message (MSG) says, "That will be the day when seven women will gang up on one man, saying, 'We'll take care of ourselves, get our own food and clothes. Just give us a child. Make us pregnant so we'll have something to live for!"

It's women like Michele who have been called to blaze the trails for women who will soon find themselves, alone, without a husband or children or family. In this five book series, Michele takes us along on her journey that didn't lead to her regaining what she lost, but finding a relationship so strong, so fulfilling and so peaceful that she is an inspiration to all of us.

Much of what I read in this book, when it was first only available to women in her church, I've used to help the women in my own ministry. Each of us needs to glean the unspoken truths, wisdom and freedom that Michele has experienced and has shared with us in this dynamic book for women.

I'm honored to call Michele my friend, and it's through what she has transparently shared with us in this book that will help us each discover how we can rise above every situation He calls us to go through.

Erin Thiele
Restore Ministries International

Chapter 1

Moving Your Mountains

> "You will say to this mountain,
> 'Move from here to there,' and it will move;
> And nothing will be impossible to you."
> —Matthew 17:20

More than anything in the world, next to being more intimate with the Lord, I have this overwhelming desire to be debt free. It's that word *free* that has taken hold of me and won't let go. It's primarily due to the realization that overtakes me (at least once each day) that reminds me of what our sweet Husband, did for you and me. I've even awakened to a new revelation that our Darling didn't die just so that you and I could get into heaven when we die, but He died His death on the cross so that you and I could be set free—free from each and every single burden in your life and mine.

If that weren't enough, He broke every one of the chains of death in order that He could be with us now, right now, as our Heavenly Husband. Then included in this act of His love, His perfect love is what does the miraculous—heals our deepest wounds and sets us free from all shame and pain.

Finally finding that abundant life, then living this life the following year, has brought me closer and closer to really seeing the magnitude of the blessings that God has bestowed on each of us when He sent His only Son to die in our place: that perfect Lamb who was slain. Then allowing Him to be our Bridegroom, forgetting the warfare and focusing on just being "in love" with Him.

Hopefully you're also at the place that you're not like many Christians who are just for when He calls us all to meet Him in the sky, but that each and every single day: each morning when you wake up, every night you go to bed, you are wrapped warmly in His sweet arms of love, and every single moment in between. If not, I would encourage you to stop and read the books that come prior to this, *Finding the Abundant Life, Living the Abundant Life,* and *The Poverty Mentality.* Each of these books are courses offered free to members of Restoration Fellowship.

However, I have come to realize that most of believers, and I mean probably 99% of Christians, do not live at the level of blessings that is ours by right. My guess is that most believers simple don't know about them, because if they did, we'd each begin to tap into these blessings, just as each of us have begun to do!

Who would have ever dreamt that you could face divorce pain-free? Certainly, not me! And I am not talking about the women who are *initiating* the divorce or women who are *spitting mad* with a vengeance if divorce is filed against them. Because whether they are honest or not, even these two groups of angry divorced women often live and do their best to suppress the pain, regrets and guilt—hidden behind their anger. Yet, by learning to tap into all that the Lord had for me, based on His promises, I went through my divorce totally pain-free *and* worry-free. (If you or someone you know who is facing divorce, be sure to take advantage of the testimony I share in *Facing Divorce Again* that is also a *free* course on **LoveAtLast.com**).

Then, there are those who have gone through supernatural childbirth—pain-free!! Who would have ever thought that was possible? Certainly, not me! And though I am past childbearing years (and am no longer married) I cannot tap into this promise myself, but my children will. I am seeing to this by speaking it, and believing it; thereby increasing the faith of my daughters, which have already led to their beliefs changing. I often hear my daughters telling people that they will have pain-free and complication-free births—they're adamant about it and we have only read halfway through *Supernatural Childbirth* as I mentioned I was doing in my last book, *Poverty Mentality.*

It was while reading this book to my children that I realized many things; one, that I often have done the right thing to move mountains in my life when I didn't even know I was doing it. The same, I'm sure, is true in your life. Are there things that you have believed God for, without wavering, and they happened just as you believed they would—you just didn't know *you* were moving one of your mountains?!

That's because our *beliefs* are far above, and much stronger, than our *hopes*. "Hoping" for something certainly has to precede believing God for something, but the difference is like thinking or saying aloud "Wow, that *would* be nice" as you "hope" for something to happen, versus thinking or saying aloud "Praise God! It's about to happen!" Let me give you just one example of how this is different that Erin shared with me.

Erin said that when she found out that her brother, who lives in Japan and whose wife is a Buddhist, was going to allow her niece to come to stay with their family for a month, she told everyone "Praise God, my niece is coming over to get saved!!" Erin said, "Even though I had never spoken to my niece about the Lord or salvation, or anything else spiritual, I had no doubt that it **was** going to happen—no doubt whatsoever. What shocked me was when I shared this with *most* Christians, they made it a point to correct me by saying "Oh, that's nice, of course we all *hope* she'll get saved [emphasizing the word hope], but we don't know that for sure" to which Erin replied, "Yes, we do! You'll see; she'll be saved before she goes back home!"

Erin went onto say, "It wasn't that I had asked God specifically for her salvation either: like asking Him, "Please, Lord, bring Monica over here so we can share the Good News with her" though praying and believing specifically can be a good thing. It is just that I could *feel* it; I could *sense* it; very much due to the *suddenly* of her coming over to stay with us. In some ways, though I can't explain it, most of the women in our ministry know what I am talking about. For years, since she was a baby, our family had been praying for my brother and his family to be saved. If I spoke to him about my faith, a wall would go up a mile high. Even worse, my brother is brilliant and knows the Bible; he just doesn't believe it (yet). So, he loves to debate, but I refuse to. Years ago, I knew He was telling me to let go of this burden and to simply live my life as an epistle. My life finally got his attention.

Though I know my brother was terrified of my "converting" his daughter, God overruled and *suddenly* my niece was coming for a visit—alone. While visiting, she was curious when she woke up and walked by during our family's morning prayer meeting (she had never heard about prayer), and she was immediately intrigued that we were "talking to God." Before she went home, as I believed would happen–my niece was indeed *radically* saved, then asked to be baptized, and during her baptism, she shared her testimony to our entire church in her broken English.

Due to her beliefs, Erin's **mountain** moved. (If you'd like to read the full testimony, be sure to find this *free* course on **LoveAtLast.com**, "Salvation Stories.")

What happened to Erin's niece, Monica, was due entirely to Erin's immovable faith. It proves what our Husband told us when He was in the midst of His ministry on earth, "And Jesus answered and said to them, 'Truly I say to you, if you have faith and do not doubt, you will not only do what was done to the fig tree, but even if you say to this **mountain**, 'Be taken up and cast into the **sea**,' it **will** happen'" (Matthew 21:21).

This is not the only time Jesus said suggested this crazy notion. Another time He answered His disciples when they asked why they were unable to cast out the demons from the lunatic:

"And He said to them, 'Because of the littleness of your faith; for truly I say to you, if you have faith the size of a mustard seed, you will say to this **mountain**, 'Move from here to there,' and it will move; and nothing will be impossible to you."

Having Faith Like a Child

Most of us know that another thing Jesus told us during His ministry is that we would need faith like a child, which simply means that we don't think of the impossibilities or all that *could* go wrong; but instead, like a child, we look to our Hero knowing that He is more than able to **do** the impossible. Is your Husband your Hero?

Funny, it was about a month ago that I told my daughters while we were driving that I was going to write this book, and told them the title "Moving Mountains." Instantly they knew what my book was going to be about. Then, to my surprise, they each said that when they first heard the verse about moving a mountain, they'd tried it! How cute is that? They both said that they were so surprised when the mountain they spoke to (a tall hill near our home) didn't move, and wondered why, in their faith like a child.

Not that they asked me intentionally, but I wanted to help them with their "whys," so in my head and heart, I spoke to their Father, my Husband, for how to answer them. Immediately I knew how to help them in a gentle, loving manner. I explained that we can compare the power we hold as believers like the power that's in a car. Unless we are mature enough to drive, our heavenly Father knows not to give us the keys. Then I went on to explain that when Jesus spoke of moving mountains, He used it figuratively, and that they, without knowing they were doing it, were already learning to move the mountains in their lives and had probably moved many without even knowing it.

Throughout our lives, you and I (and our children) will face mountains; many impossible situations and frightening circumstance will loom over us. That's when we must choose to: turn back, park ourselves at the base of the mountain, climb the mountain, go around mountain, or instead believe—when we sense He is saying to—command that the mountain move. "Truly I say to you, whoever says to this **mountain**, 'Be taken up and cast into the **sea**,' and does not doubt in his heart, but believes that what he says is going to happen, it will be granted him" (Mark 11: 23).

What motivates me to no longer doubt that a mountain will move is when I know what God says about something. If He tells me in His Word something is possible, I believe it—one reason is because He also says that He, God, cannot lie. Probably the most well-known mountain that God moved that changed the way I thought, is when I read about Erin's marriage being restored. She spoke to her mountain, she immediately after Erin said she'd read in her Bible that "nothing is impossible with God" two years earlier—it was the day that RMI unofficially began, which is what has ministered to all of us and what also later helped launch my ministry and so many others too!

Once Erin told me, "Honestly, Michele, when I was first facing abandonment, at first, I honestly didn't know what to do, but I know what I *wanted* to happen. It was what I hoped for. Then, after reading a tiny book by Dr. Ed Wheat, *How to Save Your Marriage Alone,* I began to believe it could happen. It took two years of moving several smaller mountains (as a single mother of four small children) that brought me to the place for that huge mountain of separation and divorce to be cast into the sea."

God knows that without seeing the smaller mountains move, we will have trouble believing that we have the power needed to move the *really* big mountains! That's why, when hoping to move a huge mountain, like my "Mt. Everest" that is looming over me right now, a mountain of unbelievable debt, the Lord brings me before one smaller mountain after another—teaching me what I am able to do when I believe, and no longer doubt.

Just last night I had a credit card company call to encourage me to transfer my credit card debt to their card with lower interest. When he told me the amount, saying I can transfer an *entire* balance, I laughed. I told him it didn't even come close to what I needed. That little bit would not do anything! It was like someone offering me a larger shovel to dig my way through my "Mt. Everest"—ha! No sir, I need a miracle, not another method. Thanks.

Learning how to move smaller mountains finally hit me just after the Lord led me to do my income taxes this year—myself. Insane! I shared about this in my last book, Poverty Mentality, but let me tell you a briefly why this was crazy. First, I am absolutely horrible with numbers; secondly, I have a bad habit of adding or omitting zeros (not a good thing when working with the government and IRS): third, (as I mentioned in PM) my ex-husband always did our taxes (well, actually he *gathered* the information for our taxes, which always took him the first three *months* of the new year—then he would turn everything over to a *professional* CPA, who was an "expert" with non-profit organizations, who, very often, filed for an extension because our taxes were so difficult). Have I proved my point of the magnitude of moving this mountain?

No matter how many times I told my Husband these facts, however, He kept telling me that I would do them this year—simply ignoring my excuses, and then reminded me of when I filed the paperwork to get a 501(c) 3 non-profit status. When I did this crazy, ludicrous, preposterous, even comical feat, the representative from the IRS phoned **me** *basically* saying the same thing, it was: crazy, ludicrous, preposterous. She actually said she'd called to find out what *attorney* I used, and when she heard that I was attempting this impossibility, explaining to me, me, this simpleton, that most attorneys are not skilled enough to file this very complicated and in-depth request, she then went on to tell me just what the percentage was for organizations who don't qualify for a nonprofit status each year. It was something like 95%.

It's was, however, in that exact moment in time, when the facts are so real that if you look closely—your mountain will begin to teeter just waiting to see how we, who claim to be believers, will respond. Will we agree with the impossibility? Will we take time to stop to make sure it is God's will? Or will we, instead, speak the words that will move that mountain—casting it into the sea?

That day, when the IRS representative called, I spoke the words that moved that mountain, saying, "Yes, I know it is impossible but I'd like to get a tax-exempt status" and that's when the "impossible" happened—the representative from the IRS *personally* walked me through each step over the next several days, and eventually *pushed* the request through and the nonprofit status was granted.

Though I know that (at the time) it was important that we gain this non-profit status for the sake of my new ministry, and for my family, now looking back, I how this was just one part of God's bigger plan.

He wanted me to feed you this truth "feed my sheep" so in teaching you, you will be able to help others how to move the mountain in the life of the believer, to attract the attention of nonbelievers—brides who need a Husband to live their life abundantly!!

If there is one thing that will get the attention of the lost, the desperate, it is when His brides all over the world begin to have the faith to move mountains.

The question is: Will *you* be one of them?

Just don't panic—remember, He starts us out with the little mountains first!

Chapter 2

Owe No Man

"**Owe no man** anything,
but to **love** one another."
—Romans 13:8

Most of us are familiar with this chapter's opening verse found in the book of Romans. Its message to us is simply to "owe no man anything." However, very few experience its freedom. Instead of it being a message of freedom, it instead puts a burden of heaviness on most of us when we think of the amount of debt that is looming over us—a *mountain* of debt—owed everywhere!

"But Jesus was matter-of-fact: 'Yes—and if you embrace this kingdom life and don't doubt God, you'll not only do minor feats like I did to the fig tree, but also triumph over huge obstacles. This mountain, for instance, you'll tell, 'Go jump in the lake,' and it will jump. Absolutely everything, ranging from small to large, as you make it a part of your believing prayer, gets included as you lay hold of God" (Matthew 21:21–22 MSG).

Each and every burden that befalls us was designed specifically as an *opportunity* (not a burden) to gain an increased intimacy with the Lord, our Beloved, as He calls us to, "Come to Me, all who are weary and heavy-laden, and I will give you rest. Take My yoke upon you and learn from Me, for I am gentle and humble in heart, and YOU WILL FIND REST FOR YOUR SOULS. For My yoke is easy and My burden is light" (Matthew 11:28–30). What He is saying is that each and every time we find something too heavy, we are to yoke ourselves with Him. Each burden was lovingly designed for His brides to simply turn around, handing the burden to our capable Husband.

Whether or not you accept yourself as His bride, in the Bible He refers to us as His sheep. Sheep are not burden-bearers like oxen, but are simply "fearful little creatures" who need a Good Shepherd.

It was while I was encouraging my future daughter-in-law that this entire principle became so real to me. My DIL was telling me about her desire to keep working after she married to pay off her student loans, but, she said, "it seems so impossible!" As I shared with her, it's true, yes, our mountains are meant to be impossible so that instead of us foolishly trying to dig ourselves out, we will see the *impossibility* of trying. We can even acknowledge the impossibility, but then, as believers, we need to wisely give the mountain to God— the God of impossibilities!

What He says is this, "**I am** the Lord, the God of all flesh. Is anything too hard for Me?" (Jeremiah 32:27 NLV). So, when God asks you this question: "Is anything too hard for Me?" will you speak to your mountain and answer Him, "Dear God, my Master, You created earth and sky by Your great power—by merely stretching out Your arm! There is nothing YOU can't do. You're loyal in Your steadfast love to thousands upon thousands" (Jeremiah 32:17, 18a MSG)? Or will you say and profess the opposite, as most Christians do?

When I reminded my DIL that God told us to "owe no man," she said, "I know! That's what makes me feel so sick!" Rather than focusing on how He's asked us to "owe no man anything" and then come to the false conclusion that WE are expected to carry the burden of debt and work harder. Instead, He wants us to trust Him to do it for us because our burdens are always a signal that we are not yoked to Him. "For My yoke is easy and My burden is light" (Matthew 11:30).

Let us look at *owing no man* financially as huge and impossible as my DIL felt. What's even more huge and impossible is asking us to be responsible for paying the price for our sins. Why use finances as a comparison? Because throughout Scripture, God uses financial debt to help us understand our debt for our sins and every other burden in our lives—what Jesus has **paid** for—He paid it all for us! Isn't our part to *simply* believe it and accept it?!?! God helped us with the greatest impossibility of all; am I right? Now read this story regarding a man's financial debt that He used to explain our spiritual debt.

"Therefore, the kingdom of heaven is like a king who wanted to settle accounts with his servants. As he began the settlement, a man who owed him ten thousand talents was brought to him. Since he was not able to pay, the master ordered that he and his wife and his children and all that he had be sold to repay the debt.

"The servant fell on his knees before him. 'Be patient with me,' he begged, 'and I will pay back everything.' **The servant's master took pity on him,** *canceled the debt* **and let him go.**

"But when that servant went out, he found one of his fellow servants who owed him a hundred denarii. He grabbed him and began to choke him. 'Pay back what you owe me!' he demanded.

"His fellow servant fell to his knees and begged him, 'Be patient with me, and I will pay you back.'

"But he refused. Instead, he went off and had the man thrown into prison until he could pay the debt. When the other servants saw what had happened, they were greatly distressed and went and told their master everything that had happened.

"Then the master called the servant in. 'You wicked servant,' he said, 'I canceled all that debt of yours because you begged me to. Shouldn't you have had mercy on your fellow servant just as I had on you?' In anger his master turned him over to the jailers to be tortured, until he should pay back all he owed" (Matthew 18:23–34).

Most preachers use this as a message to explain why we are to forgive others, and rightfully so; however, I believe, as with most Scripture there are many other meanings to this message that our Beloved wanted to teach us. One that's very important is that of the debt we owe others, and how God chose a way to have that debt paid *for* us. When our Beloved, while on the cross, paid the price for all our mistakes, it had to include all our debt, or it's not finished. Yet we know—He paid the price for us, for everything— because we *never* could.

"He saved us, not because of any works of righteousness that we had done, but because of His own pity and mercy" (Titus 3:5 AMP). The point is this: He saved us because we couldn't save ourselves! He set it up this way so we would depend on Him. The old saying, "God helps those who help themselves" is not only stupid—it is unbiblical. Instead, He tells us in Ephesians 2:8-9 "For by **grace** you have been saved *through faith;* and that not of yourselves, it is *the gift of God;* **not as a result of works,** so that no one may boast."

It's interesting that we are only allowed to boast in two things: two things only—first, "But HE WHO **BOASTS** IS TO **BOAST** IN THE **LORD**" (2 Corinthians 10:17). The second is, boasting about our weaknesses, and for good reason, "And He has said to me, 'My grace is sufficient for you, for power is perfected in weakness' Most gladly, therefore, I will rather **boast** about **my weaknesses**, so that the *power of Christ may dwell in me"* (2 Corinthians 12:9).

It is the pride of man, that we all know, which leads to utter destruction. Thinking we can do it alone, or even to try to do it on our own, without going to Him for help, is **pride.** It is not just us being "responsible" as many foolishly think and try to make us believe. Instead of working to pay off our debt and trying to do it alone as being a "good thing" and it a sign of our maturity—when it actually proves our spiritual immaturity.

What parent doesn't know that it is the self-centered, immature little two-year-old who puts his shoes on backward but proudly wants no help!

Once again, our Heavenly Husband paid the price and made a way for us to live an abundant life, which includes being debt-free, pain-free, worry-free—since without this freedom we cannot enjoy the life that He said He overcame! "I have told you these things, so that in Me you may have [perfect] peace and confidence. In the world you have tribulation and trials and distress and frustration; but *be of good cheer* [take courage; be confident, certain, undaunted]! For I have *overcome* the world. [I have deprived it of power to harm you and have conquered it **for *you*.**]" (John 16:33 AMP).

How can any of us "be of good cheer" if we have a mountain of **debt** hanging over us?

How can any of us "be of good cheer" if we have a mountain of **physical pain** hanging over us?

How can any of us "be of good cheer" if we have a mountain of **sin** hanging over us?

How can any of us "be of good cheer" if we have a mountain of **emotional pain** hanging over us?

Having our "emotional pain gone" is a good place to build our faith as women. Have you found the secret of no more emotional pain dear one? You'll find it with the same Person where we find relief for all our worries—in Him and in His love. His love is the greatest power on earth. It's what never fails. "Above all, keep fervent in your love for one another, because **love** covers a multitude of sins" (1 Peter 4:8). Also in 1 Corinthians 13:8 He gives us a clear promise: "Love never fails," and when it's HIS love, it will set you free and move the mountain of your emotional pain.

*If you're still not free from emotional pain (which as women, is the first mountain to be moved), then I'd encourage you to go back to the first book in the Abundant Life Series, *Finding the Abundant Life* because emotional pain and baggage is too heavy to carry and leads to a host of consequences.

My Fault

What makes us believe that our Heavenly Husband will not get us out of debt? It is because of the guilt that we did it to ourselves! True, you were totally irresponsible...yes, you knew better...you should have heeded the warnings. Does that mean you are excluded from your Husband helping you? My dear sweet bride, you couldn't be any more wrong.

If this were true, then God would tell us, "Okay, here's the way things are done. The blood that my Son shed will *only* pay for the sins that you did that you didn't know were wrong—not the ones you did intentionally. The ones you did intentionally, those you knew were wrong, YOU will have to pay that debt yourself!"

Your reasoning might be saying, "Well that's fair; I *should* have to pay." But God is not a God who is fair: God is a God of justice. And more importantly, PRAISE GOD, He is a God of mercy. Mercy, which means He chooses "compassion and forgiveness shown toward us, even though it is within His power to punish or harm us" the very definition of mercy.

Think of it. He chose to bless us, the offender, with kindness and forgiveness, overcoming every power of sin over us. It is His disposition. It's His nature to be compassionate, forgiving us. And this, dear bride, should be a welcomed event since it is preventing the most unpleasant from happening—a burden. By paying for *all* our sins, even those we *deserve* to have to pay, He lifts the distress of our burden, which reminds us of who we are in Him, His bride, and proves His love for us! Oh, to be His bride keeps me in complete and utter awe!

Without the burden, we are free to give Him the love He deserves from us—the devotion of Him being first in our lives, being our First Love. Not accepting His full payment for all our burdens, the Church is unable to experience the freedom, which leads to hearing these words, "But I have this against you, that you have left your first love" (Revelations 2:4).

So then, the question is this, dearest bride, why would you or I even *attempt* to *try* to pay a debt we can't pay for, especially when He has already paid for it? Think of it like this: What if He went on ahead to the best restaurant in town and paid for you to receive an extravagant meal. But instead of accepting it and enjoying it, and then thanking Him, praising Him and falling in love with Him even more for what He has done. Instead, you tell everyone after you've eaten that you can't pay, you're in debt, and make a plan to try to pay the cost yourself?

Believe it or not, there are some who would argue that salvation is just too simplistic and that **if** the Good News were true, if people are just forgiven, they would begin abusing their freedom by sinning even more. Yet, we know this is just simply not true. We know that the opposite is actually true. Once we really understand the magnitude of what He did by paying for our sins "while we were still sinners," this understanding causes us to seek Him more and devote more of our love to Him. And in fact, due to His love, we can begin to "sin no more," because it's the natural process and it proves our love for Him—all due because of His love!

If my Husband truly paid for my debt, then that means ALL my debt—which includes my financial debts as well as any sins committed. Because if God's grace is limited to only certain things, then we are all in trouble.

Thankfully, the truth is—His grace is limitless! And since He tells us to give our burdens to Him, while at the same time telling us to *owe no man* so that we are free to love them (because how can we honestly "love" anyone we are in debt to?). Then clearly, we can believe and wait with an expectancy that our Husband will move our mountain of debt if we simply believe He will and accept it from Him just as we accepted our salvation.

"Jesus answered them, Truly I say to you, if you have faith (a firm relying trust) and do not doubt, you will not only do what has been done to the fig tree, but even if you *say* **to this mountain,** be taken up and cast into the sea, it will be done.

"And whatever you ask for in prayer, having faith and [really] believing, you will receive" (Matthew 21:21–22 AMP).

Chapter 3

Imagine

> "Now to Him who is able to do
> Immeasurably **more**
> Than all we **ask or imagine**"
> —Ephesians 3:20

More than we can imagine? Wow, now that's difficult to wrap our minds around, isn't it? Who of us hasn't had wild and incredible images of us being radically blessed? Until, of course, someone comes along to burst our bubble with words about "reality" that cause us to come back down to earth.

Yet no matter what anyone else says, the Bible says, "I pray that out of his glorious *riches* He may strengthen you with power through his Spirit in your inner being, so that Christ may dwell in your hearts through faith. And I pray that you, being rooted and established in love, may have power, together with all the saints, to grasp how wide and long and high and deep is the love of Christ, and to know this love that *surpasses* knowledge—that you may be filled to the measure of all the fullness of God.

"Now to Him who is **able** to do *immeasurably **more*** than *all* we **ask or *imagine*,** according to His power that is at work within us, to Him be glory in the church and in Christ Jesus throughout all generations, for ever and ever! Amen" (Ephesians 3:16-21 NIV).

None of us can read the Bible or listen to the testimonies of others and not come away with the ***fact*** that God can do anything, and do anything far beyond what we can imagine. Yet, being able to *imagine* it happening is where faith begins. How do we move our mountains? We have to start by *imagining* that it *can* happen!

3. Imagine

Just the other day I was telling my oldest son, who is soon to marry, that his wife will have pain-free, uncomplicated childbirths when they have children. And I was shocked when he didn't agree; he snickered. How could this young man, *my* son, who has seen countless miracles happen not readily agree? Well, unfortunately, where his faith is concerned he has also "witnessed" most of his siblings being born. Not that I was clearly suffering, and, thankfully, I am not a screamer. Ooops, I just remembered something, something I have to confess. Even though my son didn't *see* my last baby being born, he most definitely *heard* some of it.

My last baby weighed close to 12 pounds; that's 5.44 kilograms. So as a last-ditch effort on my part, I decided to scream. Not in pain, but to get my husband's attention. Though I am not happy that my children heard me scream from the other room, the fact is, my one loud scream did cause my husband to "cry out to God" which led to a supernatural "didn't push, but **GOD** pulled" birth! But the point is this: my son has seen natural childbirth first-hand; therefore, it will take a **lot** more for him to *imagine* differently for his wife.

The next part of our conversation was my son's comment about his future children when he said, "One thing is for sure, our children will be very faired-skinned since both of us are." That's when I told him to *believe* that they would have olive skin without the burden of easily burning in the sun. Again, he chuckled. Until I said, "Hey, why not? Many of our family has olive skin" and went on to list them all. His face lit up, because for the first time, he could *imagine* that this was possible! Fast forward: Not all my grandchildren are fair skinned, but most can be out in the sun and not burn, unlike their parents.

Imagining, my dear bride, is the beginning of moving a mountain. You must be able to *imagine* the mountain moved, the unimaginable happening. So, since I never imagined when I was bearing children that having a baby pain-free was even possible—therefore, it never happened.

And before I heard about RMI and read about someone else having a restored marriage, I could never have ever imagined that restoring a marriage after adultery and divorce was possible. That's why I would never have *believed* God for my own restoration, not until I heard her testimony and read about several others. Only then I believed it could happen. Soon after I began going through the book several times and looking up the verses myself, only then was I able to imagine the impossible. Then, I discovered that the next step in moving mountains is sensing something is going to happen.

Dear bride, let's make one thing clear from the beginning. If what you need to *believe God for* is something you've never heard of, something that's never mentioned in this book or in anyone else's testimony you hear, then you, dear one, have been given the privilege of being called to be a pioneer—a true trailblazer.

Do you realize that God needs people like you who will believe what no one has *seen or heard?* God is looking for incredible people like you who are willing to build a bridge of faith over the deep ravine of doubt that keeps so many of us from gaining our promises!

"Now **faith** is the **assurance** of things **hoped** for, the **conviction** of things **not seen**" (Hebrews 11:1).

Dear bride, are you a Bridge Builder?

The Bridge Builder

By Will Allen Dromgoole

An old man, going a lone highway,

Came, at the evening, cold and gray,

To a chasm, vast, and deep, and wide,

Through which was flowing a sullen tide.

The old man crossed in the twilight dim;

The sullen stream had no fears for him;

But he turned, when safe on the other side,

And built a bridge to span the tide.

"Old man," said a fellow pilgrim, near,

"You are wasting strength with building here;

Your journey will end with the ending day;

You never again must pass this way;

You have crossed the chasm, deep and wide –

Why build you the bridge at the eventide?"

The builder lifted his old gray head:

"Good friend, in the path I have come," he said,

"There followeth after me today

A youth, whose feet must pass this way.

This chasm, that has been naught to me,

To that fair-haired youth may a pitfall be.

He, too, must cross in the twilight dim;

Good friend, I am building the bridge for *him*."

Thankfully, many years ago God called Erin to be a pioneer for women, like you and me, who found themselves in a hopeless marriage that had crumbled or ceased to exist. I wondered how she was able to believe God for the impossible, since most of you know she had never once heard of a marriage (where a husband left to be with someone else) that had ever been restored.

Part of her faith, she told me, was based on witnessing her own parents' marriage being restored after they were separated for nine years. Yet, I believe it started further back. On one of our many visits together, Erin once told me she was faced with something significant when she was just thirteen years old, something that altered the course of her life. She and her best friend were talking about the blue-eyed, blonde hair baby boys each would have after they married, and it's interesting to me what Erin determined to believe and imagine.

Erin's Blue Eyes Testimony

When I was 13-years-old my friend and I would imagine getting married, then talk about the children we would have. We both decided, as 13-years-old do, that we would have boys first. And I went on to say that my little boys would have blonde-hair and blue eyes! I could honestly *see* my little towhead boy in my mind just as clearly as if I were looking at my son Dallas and his adorable baby pictures today. It wasn't difficult for my friend to believe the same since she had blonde hair and blue eyes. Yet having dark hair and brown eyes didn't alter what I hoped for. A baby boy with blonde hair and blue eyes is what I wanted, so I imagined it and spoke about it often for years.

Later, when I was in college, I began as a premed student, which meant that one of my classes was genetics. In it we were asked to conduct a personal research. I chose to research the chances of my children having certain characteristics based on genetics, statistics, and gene strengths. Of course, since it was my dream to have a blue-eyed child, I based my research on this statistic. Since my eyes are brown, I discovered my odds were not good. I had, in fact, only a 1 in 4 possibility of having a blue-eyed child—and **only if**: I married someone who had blue eyes. In addition, for this 1 in 4 chance, both his parents would have to have blue eyes, and at least one of my parents would have to have blue eyes. Unfortunately, *neither* of my parents had blue eyes.

Nevertheless, I had more than statistics on my side. I had a mother of faith who told me that when she was a little girl her father had all of her dolls' eyes changed from the normal blue to brown. She said she *prayed* for brown-eyed babies, and she got seven of them! True, brown eyes are dominant, but I just knew, like my mother, He would give me the desires of my heart.

Even though I saw what my paper concluded, that it was an impossibility, and I received an "A" for my research to confirm that what I hoped for was impossible, I simply prayed and believed that when I had children I would have a blonde haired, blue-eyed baby boy. And because the visions of having that little boy were stronger than facts—the result of me being able to imagine and believe resulted in—my first three children were boys with blonde hair AND blue eyes! And, for years everyone made sure to tell me my first son's eyes would change color, but they never did. As a matter of fact, they are just as blue today as they were when he was a baby, and he is complimented on just how blue they are all the time!

By the way, the chances of having a blonde-haired child were better, since 5 out of my 6 siblings were blonde when they were young—but it was still a long shot because both their father and I were born with dark hair.

It was after my last baby, when my daughter Macy was born, who still has blonde hair and blue eyes that I fully realized that God can do anything—more than we could imagine or hope for. Just like it says in Ephesians 3:20 TLB, "Now glory be to God, who by his mighty power at work within us is able to do far more than we would ever dare to ask or even dream of—infinitely beyond our highest prayers, desires, thoughts, or hopes."

So now my dear bride, after reading Erin's testimony, what sort of things have you desired and maybe even imagined but were afraid to really hope for? I am sure if you're like me, there are hundreds of things that you may have never even spoken about or haven't spoken about in a very long time.

Today is the day to set aside a special time to talk to your Heavenly Husband. Talk to Him about your deepest most innermost treasures of your heart and pull them out one-by-one, and ask Him if you should let go or begin to believe and imagine and not give up on them happening. It is not too late for any of them, but if you have outgrown the impossibility, like I have for a pain-free childbirth, because you're past childbearing years, be sure you pass the impossibility on to the next generation!

"'For I know the *plans* I have for you,' says the Lord, 'plans for **well-being** and *not* for trouble, to give you a *future* and a *hope*'" (Jeremiah 29:11 NLV).

"Therefore the LORD *longs* to be **gracious** to you, and therefore He waits on high to have compassion on you For the LORD is a God of justice; how blessed are all those who long for Him" (Isaiah 30:18).

"Instead of your shame you will have a *double portion,* and instead of humiliation they will shout for joy over their portion Therefore they will possess a *double portion* in their land, everlasting joy will be theirs" (Isaiah 61:7).

"There is no fear in love; but **perfect love** *casts out fear...*" (1 John 4:18).

"*Ask Me* about the things to come..." (Isaiah 45:11). "Your ears will hear a word behind you, 'This is the way, walk in it,' whenever you turn to the right or to the left" (Isaiah 30:21).

Just be sure to "think on" each of these promises, so you can then begin to IMAGINE the impossible!!

Chapter 4

Promises

> "Let us hold on to the **hope** we say
> we have and not be changed.
> We can trust God that He will do
> what He **promised**."
> —Hebrews 10:23 NLV

What we say, everything that we allow to come out of our mouths, has to be one of the most important characteristics of a godly woman. Most of us learned this truth from reading *How God Can and Will Restore Your Marriage* or reading *A Wise Woman* by Erin Thiele. We learned that the enemy has used the area of communication to undermine and destroy many women and their relationships. And I can attest that, like many of you, this is what destroyed mine.

In the same books, most of us could relate to (and know first-hand) that counselors and so-called marriage "experts" still continue to tell us that it is a ***lack* of communication** that destroys our relationships. Yet, again, when searching the Scriptures after reading Erin's book, you will find, as she did, as I did, that God tells us over and over again the exact opposite.

It's in this chapter that I will share with you even more truth about communication, which goes beyond relationships. We must hold on to the hope we say we have and not allow anything to change or vary it, lest we find ourselves robbed of so much more than we could have imagined.

There are so many Christians who never make it past the level of hoping for something, or maybe they only allow themselves to imagine for just a moment that something they long for will happen.

This is due to an inability to comprehend the true nature of God—the God who can be trusted if what you desire is something that He has promised.

"So let's do it—full of belief, confident that we're *presentable inside and out*. Let's keep a firm grip on the promises that keep us going. He *always* keeps His word" (Hebrews 10:23 MSG).

Deep within the message of this verse above, we see something that often keeps us from asking for and believing God's promises—even when we know what His word says. Are *you* "confident that you're presentable inside and out"? What's keeping us from believing is often due to feeling that we are *unworthy,* and this is what keeps us from asking and believing God for something wonderful. We think to ourselves, "If others only knew what I am like," and we allow the enemy to convince us that we are far from "presentable."

Has this ever plagued you? I am sure it has, because the schemes of the enemy are always the same—first and foremost because so many of his schemes work. Honestly, who of us is worthy of receiving anything at all? Certainly not me! And if I were to think myself worthy, then I would be suffering from a serious condition known as pride! Humility is walking out the belief that we *are* unworthy while still having the knowledge that, by His grace and mercy, He has provided us first and foremost with His salvation, not just when we die, but right now. In addition, we understand that He also died to give us an abundant life in this world, not just in the next. Therefore, the question is not whether we are worthy. The question is: Are we willing to allow one drop of the precious blood that Jesus shed to fall unused?

"Therefore the LORD *longs* to be **gracious** to you, and therefore He waits on high to have compassion on you; For the LORD is a God of justice; how blessed are all those who long for Him" (Isaiah 30:18 MEV). If you are longing for Him and what He has died to give you—then you can rest in His promises. However, if you are longing for what His hand can give you, the things of this world, then it's quite possible you have missed the promise altogether.

"I came that they may have life, and **have it abundantly.** I am the Good Shepherd. The Good Shepherd lays down His life for the sheep" (John 10:10-11 ESV).

If you are a mom, you know how you feel about giving to your children. We have this insatiable desire to give everything to our children, in spite of our own sinful human nature. So just think how much more God *longs* to bless us and how He hurts when we refuse His blessings. "If you then, being evil, know how to **give good gifts** to your children, how much more will your Father who is in heaven **give** what is **good** to those who ask Him!" (Matthew 7:11).

Recently, for me to fully understand the hurt that our Father feels when we reject His blessings (gifts that Jesus actually died to give us), the Lord has seen fit for me to live *through* some extremely painful things. If you have already read my book *Poverty Mentality* (which is the third book in the "Abundant Life" series), then you know how difficult it was for me when my daughter refused to allow me to buy her a car, with cash. Even now her car has been a huge burden, because she denied the blessing that ultimately came from God. It showed me just a glimpse of how we mess up our lives and live in a state of poverty. We enter into lack, simply because we will not look for and accept the blessings that Jesus died to give us— longing to bless us.

Though that incident was difficult, the one that I most recently lived through was so hard that right now I am having trouble writing about it, because the wounds are so fresh. However, this too gives me a glimpse of His nail-scarred hands and spear-pierced side. It helps me come to grips with the fact that our Husband was and is our example. As it says in First Peter, "For you have been called for this purpose, since Christ also suffered for you, leaving you an example for you to follow in His steps . . . and while being reviled, He did not revile in return; while suffering, He uttered no threats, but kept entrusting Himself to Him [God] who judges righteously" (1 Peter 2:21–23). This proves He knows our pain firsthand, and it explains why He is so understanding as a husband, living with us "in an understanding way," as we are "the weaker vessel," since we are women, and why He bestows honor on us daily. (See 1 Peter 3:7 ESV.)

Once again, if you read my book *Poverty Mentality,* you also read the incredible and miraculous testimony about my son's honeymoon to Hawaii. It was a miracle that left me soaring like an eagle; yet, would you believe that just weeks before the wedding I received a phone call, late one evening, from my son who simply said, "We decided not to go"? Let me be honest and tell you that at first it was such a shock that I had trouble comprehending it (and so did others who heard about it later). It hurt. It honestly broke my heart, and it left me more than a little bit bewildered.

It took time and tears in my prayer closet to come out with the peace and assuredness that I could **trust the Lord** and that somehow, in someway, He would work it out for good—though, at the time, I could not really imagine how He could. May I tell you that, even during your darkest hours, He is more than able to bless you and move mountains that you never think need to be moved? Well, He really can, but it takes trusting Him and His promises to unleash those blessings that are even more than you believe or imagine.

Like I am in the habit of doing, I simply claimed one of my absolute favorites verses, Romans 8:28, and it was that verse alone that unleashed the most powerful mountain moved that I have even experienced in my life! All things *can* work together for good, as long as we honestly love Him above all else and are called according to His purpose—allowing it to happen!

Though everyone tried to convince me to cancel the vacation, there was really no point. I could not get those thousands of flying miles back, nor get any of the points returned from the resort, and the cost of the rental car seemed a bit trivial in comparison to the thousands of dollars that the honeymoon cost. And what mattered to me was not the cost at all, but it was that my gift was (for some reason) rejected. This has led me to understand more fully how He feels when we fail to accept His gifts for us. We all, as Christians, are amazed when we hope to lead someone to the Lord, and then that person rejects the gift of salvation—we simply don't understand, do we?

Though my flesh wanted to hide the folder (that contained the documents they needed to bring with them on their honeymoon), the Lord had spoken to me that I needed to leave it out in plain view. Each time I saw the folder, I simply said, "I trust You," but I confess it still hurt. And though I never shared what happened, that the honeymoon was cancelled, the word got out (maybe their brother told them). Even my effort to be discreet had been overridden. But it's when my other children heard what had happened, specifically when my oldest son, who was also engaged, heard, that motivated him to try to do "something"—but he tried in his "own strength."

It's just like the picture of the woman on the cover of this *Moving Mountains* book; it's foolish for any of us to attempt to move a mountain that is immovable. Ultimately, even though his heart was right, the effort left him frustrated and worn out, because it was "he" who tried to move it. Nevertheless, as I said, it showed the heart of my son, which proved to be a blessing, since not only did I see it, but so did the Lord, who was able to reward him accordingly!

My son and his fiancé are a precious couple; however, they are both extremely talented and mentally capable of so much, which is why they can easily attempt to do everything in their own strength. Therefore, He often chooses to hem each of us in, in order to show us just how much He loves us and how much He can do when He is given the opportunity.

Let me also say to those of us who are obsessed with the fact that we are always running out of time, let's remember that *time* is not a part of God's make up. He was, is, and will always be. I know this concept is something far beyond what we truly can comprehend, but it simply means, God, on purpose, moves suddenly, yet often waits until the very last minute—and very often He *appears* to be late—just as He was when He allowed Lazarus to die in order for him to be raised from the dead.

So, as is His very nature, God continued to tell me to **trust Him,** and then with time running out, suddenly, the Monday before the Saturday flight, there appeared in the sky a cloud, the size of a man's fist—"The seventh time the servant reported, 'A cloud as small as a man's hand is rising from the sea.' So Elijah said, 'Go and tell Ahab, 'Hitch up your chariot and go down *before the rain stops you*'" (1 Kings 18:44 NIV).

My son's fiancé called to tell me something "interesting." She said that when she told her mother about the horrible honeymoon situation, she told her mom that if they (as a couple) could take the trip, they would, so that I wouldn't lose anything. Her mom responded by saying, "Darling, if this happens—it's God! Do it!" My son's fiancé went on to say that she responded to her mom that even if it did work, neither of them had any cash (money for food, gas, etc. for the trip), but then her mom had reminded her that she gave them a thousand dollars for her wedding and that should be more than enough!

When I heard this, I told my son's fiancé that "ready or not," they were about to take that trip as **her** honeymoon! Though my son had tried before, I know how God works, and I knew that this tiny cloud meant that very soon there would be a downpour of blessings!!

Then, the test happened. When my son's fiancé called, she said my son's response was that they shouldn't try. This is what happens when we try things in our own strength—we feel there is no use in trying again. So she called me back and, to me, she passed her test with an A+, when she said, "Mom, your son is about to be my spiritual leader; he always has to be. So, since he said "no," I can't say another word. But what should I do? What do I do with these feelings that I believe God wants to do this and that I want so much?" Oh my, even now, what she said brings me to tears: that this precious girl will allow my son to lead her, and that she is asking ME for guidance. Though I may not deserve to be so blessed, I am going to accept this blessing from Him!

In seeking my HH guidance, I answered by saying that this was a promise for her and it was meant to hide in her heart, just as Mary, the mother of Jesus did. I assured her that Mary was certainly a wonderful wife to Joseph, so she hid the tender things in her heart to ponder. I told her to trust that if this was God's will, He would turn her future husband's heart. I said, I too, would hide everything we imagined in my heart. How I felt or how my son's fiancé felt, of course, was not my place to discuss with my son, who is being called to lead his wife (and very soon, I hope, his family) spiritually. Within the hour, my son called me to say, "Mom, this trip to Hawaii is something that I can tell my bride really wants; what can I do to make it happen?" Hallelujah, thank you Lord!! I said, "Let's just begin to imagine this mountain is starting to move!"

Once you see that God is calling you to believe and imagine a mountain moving, there are two things that you need to know: one, don't worry about what you *can't* do, and two, just **do** what you *can, as He leads you!*

"The Lord is my Shepherd, I shall not want. He makes me lie down in green pastures; **He leads me** beside quiet waters. He restores my soul" (Psalm 23:1-3).

When the Lord **led** me to do my own taxes (something only a well-trained professional with an expertise in non-profit ministry should attempt), each time I came up against a brick wall (or the side of a mountain that wouldn't budge), the Lord told me to look for something I *could* do. As crazy as this may seem, at least three times while doing my taxes the only thing I *could* do was to fill out my name on yet another form! But, somehow, and for some reason, it **led** me to keep going until, miraculously—it all got done!!

This is what I told my son, who then asked, "Okay, what CAN I do?!" Immediately I asked Him for the answer, and out of my mouth I asked my son "where" he was going to get married. When he first tried to make this honeymoon happen, they'd planned to get married here, then fly out on Saturday for their honeymoon. But now there clearly was no time. So his response was, "Well, I guess we can get married there, in Hawaii; we'll have a destination wedding!!" So I told him to find out for sure if this was possible, if there was any waiting period, etc. When I hung up, I then asked the Lord what I *could* do. He led me to open the honeymoon folder that once brought heartache and now brought hope and expectancy, and He showed me there were three parts to this miracle: the flight, the resort, and the rental car.

The Lord prompted me to start with the resort. Expecting to sit on hold for at least thirty minutes, and sometimes as long as an hour, in awe I was connected to a "person" immediately. Less than ten minutes later, the "non-transferable" reservation was in the name of my oldest son!! The mountain was sliding closer to the sea...

Let me interject something that I believe you will find most interesting. Before I called the resort, the Lord led me to read the bottom of the letter of confirmation; there, in big bold letters, I read that the reservations were non-transferable, non-changeable—in other words, it was *impossible* to make any and all changes! Yet, He did not stop there. When I looked at it, I held it up in comparison to the God of impossibilities. This is another key to unleashing the power to move mountains and what we learned from our father Abraham.

The principle is found in one of my ultimate favorite portions of the Bible. Here is what it says, "In hope against hope he [Abraham] believed...Without becoming weak in faith he *contemplated* his own body, now as good as dead since he was about a hundred years old, and the deadness of Sarah's womb; **YET,** with respect to the promise of God, he did not waver in unbelief but grew strong in faith, giving glory to God, and being fully assured that what God had promised, He was able also to perform" (Romans 4:18-21). Abraham didn't ignore the impossibility of his having a son with his deadening body and Sarah's dead womb; he didn't pretend, but instead, it says he "contemplated" this fact, but then he determined to compare the facts to God's promises, and His ability to perform what He promised!!

When the Lord showed me the bolded, in all caps, laws (if you will) of these reservations, I already knew that nothing was impossible with God and that, because He wrote our laws, therefore, He can overturn them if He chooses to! In the exact same way, the Lord went on to show me the "no-cancellation policy statement" on the rental car, which quite honestly seemed minuscule and hardly worth my time, but again, He wanted to teach me something: always *ask*.

When I got online, I *asked* Him what I should do, and He answered me in bold red letters right there on the page; when I began to type in the confirmation number, it actually popped up, "Do you want to cancel this rental car?" When my eyes jumped up to my second son's name, I immediately said, "Yes" and clicked! Then I *asked* the Lord what I should do next, when it actually said in red letters, all caps, "Do you want to rent another car?" to which I yelled, "Yes!!" and proceeded to rent the exact same car, same pick up date, same everything—only the first name was changed to my other son and the payment transferred over!

Too often, we lose connection with the Lord when we start moving the mountains in our lives. So be sure to continue to ask the Lord after each step you make, and don't panic if it seems you made a wrong turn. Just ask again.

With two parts down, I could now see and feel the mountain teetering; just one more push and that mountain, and all it stood for, was about to slip neatly into the depths of the sea!! It happened just a few hours later, when I got a call from my son's fiancé, who told me excitedly that my son was standing in line at the airport to speak directly to the airline. I was beside myself with joy and expectancy; since I had a vision of my son in line at the airport just days earlier—this, to me, was the confirmation that the final step was about to happen!

Even before anything happened, I was so excited that I hurried to tell my other children (all who have faith like a child) to rejoice with me, that the miracle was about to happen. I just knew that I knew that I knew that it was going to happen in an instant; therefore, I began to act as if it had already happened! "Therefore I tell you, whatever you ask for in prayer, believe that you have received it, and it will be yours" (Mark 11:24 NIV).

About an hour later, I got a call from my son. He was on his way home, and he told me that the airline had tried and tried, but the fields to be able to make any changes were blocked. The airline said that the only people who could make a change would be the booking agent where I used my flying miles. Though my feelings wanted to plummet, and so did his, I told him that there was a reason, and this would simply be "the next step." So, I hung up and quickly made the call, only to find that they had closed; we missed them by just ten minutes.

Waiting was good; it strengthens us spiritually, so, I told my son that this setback was all part of His plan, and I sensed that He needed to show me "something." Sitting there quietly in my room, He had me pick up that infamous folder again. With my faith soaring, my Husband led me to read again the very fine print on the same document, this time online. It began the same, stating in bold that reservations were non-transferable, no changes, etc. etc., **but then,** I saw something paragraphs down. There it went on to say, deep within the paragraph in tiny, tiny print, that if the airline approved of a change, then we were to contact them first! There it was; it was written; that was it— now all I had to do was wait until morning.

Again, setbacks only prove that the Lord needs to show us something else. In this instance, He wanted us to speak to someone who would be working the next morning with the truth posted on their site. When a mountain is huge and immovable, He asks us to believe that everything, even setbacks and brick walls, are all part of His plan. Rather than falling apart and allowing setbacks to weaken your faith, use them to your advantage by *knowing* that they are just another part of your testimony, part of His plan, and He's going to move that mountain that has been grounded in your heart.

That night I fell asleep quickly but woke at 4 A.M. Not only were those four hours while I waited for the office to open at 8 not wasted, they proved to build my excitement and expectancy, as the Lord led me to write earlier chapters of this book, building my faith in His ability and desire to move this mountain, as I spoke it and believed!

Watching the last three minutes click by, I was literally trembling with excitement. (Mind you, my emotions wanted to take hold of me in the form of fear, which we will discuss in more detail in chapter 9.) When I finally made the call that morning, the Lord reminded me of how the "way of no resistance and cheerfulness" had worked so miraculously the day before with the telephone company. (You will learn about this principle in chapter 8.)

Sure enough, the first person I spoke to assured me that it was *impossible,* then proceeded to try to sell me something. Oh my, this is when our emotions want to jump out of our skin (and out our mouths). That's the real challenge, dear bride. We must continue to stay peaceful, agreeable and not let haste or hurry, which leads to panic, take over. This, too, I learned while doing my taxes. I had to stay in perfect peace in order to hear His still small voice. Even in the midst of dogs barking, telephone calls, and children interrupting me asking trivial questions, I had to remain joyful and peaceful, if I wanted to move a mountain using His strength.

So, patiently, and in full excitement, I listened to the woman's sales pitch excitedly, for what I knew would still happen, thankfully, when she stopped. I was able to *kindly* tell her I had just purchased what she was selling, which led her to say, "Hey, wait a minute; let me see if they might be able to help you in another department," and she transferred me. Without going through each of the next *seven* people I talked to, how each person gave me the same "impossible" response, followed by my agreeable "that's okay" and being transferred to "someone else" who "might" be able to help, I, finally, was connected to the top person in the flying miles company, who assured me that the *airline* had the *power to change* the details of the flight and gave me their number to allow me to "try."

Throughout this whole ordeal, I was told the same thing: what I desired, what I believed could happen, was impossible, and that, if allowed (what they wouldn't allow), the points would have to be first refunded (which they don't do), new tickets would then have to be booked, and everything would have to be re-ticketed. In other words, we would have to start from scratch, which, by this late date, *would* be impossible.

However, we know that nothing is impossible with God. "Behold, I am the LORD, the God of all flesh; is anything too difficult for Me?" (Jeremiah 32:27). And I answered Him, "Ah Lord GOD! Behold,

You have made the heavens and the earth by Your great power and by Your outstretched arm! Nothing is too difficult for You"! (Jeremiah 32:17).

Who of us hasn't heard Erin's testimony? When years ago, way back in 1989, Erin told the Lord that if He did the impossible by restoring her marriage—a marriage with a man who left her for another woman, divorced her, and said he would never come back to her because he didn't love her and never did—then she would spend her life telling the world that nothing was impossible for Him.

Back then, I embraced this true for my own marriage, and since that time God has given me the impossibilities, impossibilities that continually sweeten my life and continue to prove that it is TRUE—nothing, not one thing, is impossible with God!

When I contacted the airline, in an instant I heard the lady on the phone tell me to hold while she CHANGED THE NAMES! What?!?! We in the United States have been told since 9/11 that changing the names was illegal. So, I sat on hold for more than 20 minutes, with about four, five-minute intervals when she came on to thank me for my patience, saying, "sorry, this is just something that we NEVER do, so I really don't know how exactly to do it"! It was after her second reassurance that tears welled up in my eyes, my heart beating out of my chest—I was watching my mountain, the one that had caused me so much pain, fall into the sea! I began to weep.

Then, right after the third reassurance, when she told me that they were "almost done," I jumped up from my chair to dance with the Lord and pulled my back out, completely. All I could do was laugh—and, gingerly, I sat back down in pain. But my heart was soaring.

When she thanked me and we hung up, I was stunned, crying, shaking, all as I tried to call my son. Screaming, I told him that God did the impossible! My children woke up that morning to my screams of delight, as they ran in and began dancing around with me—their brother was getting married in Hawaii, how romantic—God had moved a mountain of impossible proportion!

"Behold, I have made you a new, sharp threshing sledge with double edges; you will thresh the mountains and pulverize them, and will make the hills like chaff" (Isaiah 41:15).

"Jesus said to them [when the apostles were baffled because they were not able to cast a demon out], 'Because you have so little faith. For sure, I tell you, if you have faith as a mustard seed, you will say to this mountain, 'Move from here to over there,' and it would move over. You will be able to do anything'" (Matthew 17:20 NLV).

Dear bride, before reading the next chapter, stop to consider why He led you to read this chapter and its truths. There is no question that there is one specific mountain in your life that He wants to move, until He casts a whole range of mountains that have shadowed your life. Remember, it begins with one small mountain—but a mountain nonetheless. Ask Him which it is, and then begin to ask what He wants you to do. Even if He says to wait, believe, imagine, hide it in your heart— and I promise that soon you will begin to move mountains; nothing is impossible with Him.

Chapter 5

Baby Steps

"We **walk** by faith,
Not by sight"
—2 Corinthians 5:7

Most Christians don't understand, and therefore they are unable to walk the walk of faith. I believe that this is merely due to the fact that they don't fully comprehend the blessings of walking the walk of faith, which is accomplished primarily by doing so in the dark, taking tiny baby steps as they go.

It says that we should, "Trust in the LORD with all your heart and do not lean on your own understanding. In all your ways acknowledge Him, and He will make your paths straight. Do not be wise in your own eyes" (Proverbs 3:5–7). To me, this verse sums it up beautifully: we have no idea where we are going or what is up ahead, and because of this, we should not foolishly think we do. Unfortunately, it seems that the majority of Christians have a pattern and have fallen into the rut, which is simply to pray about a way *they* **want** to go, then when any door opens, they *run through it,* without taking His hand. Our HH wants to guide each of us— every baby step of the way!

It is certainly true, however, that there are those who know and abide in His Word, who have the advantage and often walk with great wisdom. The result is steps that appear more as running, no longer the baby steps that you or I might need to take. "I have directed you in the way of wisdom; I have led you in upright paths. When you walk, your steps will not be impeded; and if you *run,* you will not stumble" (Proverbs 4:11–12).

5. Baby Steps   41

However exciting, even steps of wisdom cannot compare to taking the walk of your life, which means taking baby steps in the dark while He holds your hand and guides you. "Yes, though I walk through the [deep, sunless] valley of the shadow of death, I will fear or dread no evil, *for You are with me;* Your rod [to protect] and Your staff [to guide], they comfort me" (Psalm 23:4 AMP). True, walking in the dark often feels scary, especially when you have not truly experienced the very nature of our Husband and His love—which will be totally and completely "**perfect**" because "**perfect love** *casts out fear.*" That's because, "Such love has no fear, because perfect love expels ***all*** fear. If we are afraid, it is for fear of punishment, and this shows that we have not fully experienced His perfect love" (1 John 4:18 NLT).

So many Christians are honestly *afraid* to trust God with their future, even their day-to-day future, because they believe if they simply give their future to Him, He will ask them to do things that are too hard or something they wouldn't like. This leads to missed opportunities, when each could have experienced the abundant life He died to give each of us. I am no exception. Even though I have lived an incredibly unbelievable life, I still tend to pull back when faced with walking boldly when He calls. Take for instance traveling around the world: I met and experienced things that no one could ever imagine, even I can't believe I really lived it, and yet, when my new passport came, I cringed, thinking that He might call me to begin traveling again. We are all the same, aren't we? We simply are fearful little sheep in desperate need of a loving and patient Shepherd.

Do you know that it is because of our fear, our trepidation and our hesitancy, that the Lord causes us to wait, on purpose? I have seen it time and again in my life and in the lives of my children (my own and my spiritual ones). So often the Lord will show us something, then He makes us wait for it (long past the time that we *thought* it should take). Only then will He open the door so that we do what comes naturally: pull back or bolt. "O LORD, be gracious to us; we have *waited* for You. Be their strength every morning, our salvation also in the time of distress" (Isaiah 33:2). And "Yet those who *wait* for the LORD will gain new strength; they will mount up with wings like eagles, they will run and not get tired, they will walk and not become weary" (Isaiah 40:31).

For the past few months, my son has been waiting for a new position, waiting as they complete the hiring process for his new job. The main reason for the wait was for him to see that it *was* God. Initially, he could see that it was God's plan, since they actually sought him for the position, and it's in the city where his fiancée lived, where he always wanted to live, but all too soon he began *saying* that he wasn't sure he even wanted the job.

It took God bringing him to a place of financial ruin for him to see that having a base salary, rather than waiting for clients to pay as he'd been doing, would be what a new marriage needed (not to mention long hours, often working through the night). Thankfully, the Lord gave me at least two opportunities to confirm these words of wisdom with my son (for the sake of his future wife), to confirm that His plan was accomplished—all due to the long, and very unusual, wait to hear he had gotten the position. [He is still in this position after 10 years.]

Each and every day, I see the Lord faithfully renewing *my* strength by causing me to wait for something. Even though having to wait for something is what our entire family is known for; nevertheless, waiting never comes easily, *even* when you are accustomed to it. It was just yesterday, more than a week from when my son left to get married, when I finally got to see any wedding pictures. I just wanted to see a picture of my son married. Honestly, though I have learned daily how to wait, waiting for just one picture was really tough. Though I could have emailed them to ask, or left a message on one of their cell phones, or done some other less-than-gracious attempt to get a picture that other parents might have done, I knew that the fact that it did not come had nothing to do with them—but everything to do with me. As I said, the Lord faithfully sees fit to continually renew my strength—because the Lord knows I need it. And believe it or not, so do you. Does that help you understand, just a bit better, why you have not heard from someone or about something or have

5. Baby Steps

not received something promised—long past when you should have heard or received it?

Baby steps in the dark are what I am trying to encourage my older children to take, especially the ones who are now married. When they ask for advice, I simply encourage them to ask the Lord what to do next. However, all of us want a full and expansive plan that looks well into the future. Unfortunately, if we really knew how it all worked out, no doubt it would cause many of us to run ahead, or, more than likely, to turn and run away! Honestly, if I had known even one percent of what was up ahead in my life over the past twenty years, I would have found my own way of escape—hardly an example of a wise woman who smiles at the future. Instead, I have learned that, like the story of the slow-moving tortoise and the fast-moving hare, the way to moving mountains is by slow and careful steps, as we ask, believe, and then move in the direction He is leading us, all while holding His hand during the process.

By the way, moving slowly is not my nature at all, just so that you understand that I do indeed understand how you feel. From the time I was young, my motto was that "I was a sprinter;" I was not "a long-distance runner." However, for this race of our life, we must have endurance, which is only available to those who are willing to wait. And then He asks us, as His bride, to take tiny baby steps through that dark, deep valley, all the while holding the hand of the Shepherd, who is also, for many of us, our beloved Husband.

My dear, if you are also facing life alone right now (without a husband or with a husband who does not believe), then you know that this walk of faith is especially disconcerting: uneasy and confusing, while leaving you feeling a bit dismayed. Nevertheless, "Give glory to the LORD your God, before He brings darkness and before your feet to stumble on the dusky mountains, and while you are hoping for light He makes it into deep darkness, and turns it into gloom" (Jeremiah 13:16). Thankfully your journey does not need to be gloomy, not if you keep your eyes looking into His face, as you take the next baby step.

"For You have delivered my soul from death, indeed my feet from stumbling, so that I may walk before God in the light of the living" (Psalm 56:13). Because "Your word is a lamp to my feet and a light to my path" (Psalm 119:105).

The only way I will ever be able to move the mountain of debt, which I set out to do when I first started this book, is by taking each baby step, one-by-one. Nothing that you face now is insignificant, but each step is God-ordained. Had I not first tackled my taxes, I would not have known the power of remaining calm at all times—in order to move a mountain. Just two days ago, I did just the opposite, which proved how powerful and necessary this principle of remaining calm is to moving mountains.

Remain Calm

We had a house full of guests for my son's wedding reception, and I served our guests a formal dinner with the help of my children. They were enjoying themselves, as we all love to do, now that the oppression in our home is gone after the divorce, and they were dancing on the dance floor, while I was trying to get the food served to our guests. Right after I called to them the second time, I found *stress* began to overwhelm me. As a result, for about ten or fifteen minutes, I lost my peace, and more importantly, my joy! No, I did not yell or anything. It's just that I had lost my usual "joyful bliss" (the constant overwhelming joy in my heart) that I have come to enjoy and savor. The lack of patience caused one problem after another, until I shook off the stress and regained the composure of walking peacefully in the spirit—then everything began to change almost magically: clearly supernaturally.

Not only had it affected my composure and joy, but the following day when I commented to my son, who had been in charge of grilling our food, on how wonderfully things had turned out, he commented with a half-hearted "yes." Without realizing it, he had felt *my* stress, which had affected his own enjoyment during the event and his memory of it. This is another good lesson for us all: never underestimate how an interruption in our peaceful emotions can affect the people who we love the most.

5. Baby Steps

Baby steps, for me, were as simple as learning to be "joyfully agreeable," which I learned while I was married, then I used this same principle with my telephone company: agreeing that it was *my* fault and that the charges for the last three months (that were twice the usual amount) were no problem at all for me to pay. Without those tiny steps, I would not have seen how easily the spirit of non-resistance changes the entire spiritual energy in a conversation, for my good. Remaining peaceful is what led me to do the same thing the very next day, with the flying miles company, that finally led me to the right person at the airline, who had the authority to change the names on the tickets to Hawaii, that I spoke about in an earlier chapter.

Even the tiniest baby steps of not trying to fix the telephone bill weeks earlier paid off, because how to do it His way was fresh in my mind. He knew when I would really need to know how to deal with opposition—so He made me wait!

Though we all want to make progress and take great strides toward moving our mountains, the only way to move a mountain is to begin with one small baby step, nothing grand or of real importance. Aren't we all still amazed, as were the apostles, when Jesus simply "spoke" to the storm to be still? He was not overwhelmed and stressed, but He remained calm, because He, above all, knew the truth and the power of doing things in accordance with the way God had created the universe. God's way is not flashy in the technique, but the results *are* magnificent and awesome when manifested simply!

Remember, for instance, how He chose to heal the blind: once by spitting on the ground, then making a paste, which is not something too spectacular, until we witness the result. And even before Jesus came to earth, not dipping seven times in murky water would have meant that a man (Naaman) would have died from leprosy, instead of being able to walk away the way he did, whole and healed, due to the simplicity of Elijah's instructions.

Just today, I was reminded of the significance of baby steps and waiting for His timing, when I *felt like* calling a furniture store which had promised to deliver a couple of pieces of furniture I purchased well over a week ago. Yet, my HH told me to wait, to be patient. So, now I know it's not about the "incompetent" furniture company but rather the means the Lord chose to use to train me even more—how to learn more about the blessings of waiting and the significance of it in relation to moving mountains. And again, today, I ended up speaking to my children a couple of times about situations in which, despite me being curious, I had *not asked* any details, and as a matter of fact, I had specifically told them not to tell me. Yet, in both of these instances, months later, the details were revealed that confirmed a direction that the Lord had called me to take. Do you also find this interesting?

How would I sum up this chapter, so that it teaches us, you and me, about the significance and importance of taking small and guided baby steps? It is this: nothing you do is unimportant, nothing. And doing it in the proper timing is also extremely important. This is only possible, as you and I know, from learning to wait, which in itself is a baby step.

Baby steps also have to be done blindly, with no guarantees. Our only guarantee is the One who has made us the promises: that mountains will be moved, when we come to the place of faith where we no longer doubt.

"But Jesus was matter-of-fact: 'Yes—and if you embrace this kingdom life and don't doubt God, you'll not only do minor feats like I did to the fig tree, but also triumph over huge obstacles. This mountain, for instance, you'll tell, 'Go jump in the lake,' and it will jump. Absolutely everything, ranging from small to large, as you make it a part of your believing prayer, gets included as you lay hold of God'" (Matthew 21:21 MSG).

Chapter 6

Opposition

> "He will speak against the Most High
> And **oppress** his saints
> And try to change the set times and the laws."
> —Daniel 7:25

You might as well face it—if you want to move a mountain in your life you are going to encounter opposition. But, the problem is not the "source or intensity of the opposition"; the problem is *how we respond to it*. Let's be honest; when opposition stands in the way of our miracle, our mountain moving, we all respond in the same way—we resist it or push against it. When we do, we are doing the complete *opposite* of what will move our mountain. What is worse is that the resistance will wear us out, so that we will all too soon give up, because this is exactly what the opposition is meant to do.

In speaking about the enemy, this verse alludes to the fact that this is one of the enemy's schemes: when it says in the book of Daniel 7:25 "He will...***wear* down** the **saints** of the Highest One." In other versions of the Bible, it says that "he will wear out, he will be cruel, he will make it hard, and he will oppress." Oppression was always something I had trouble dealing with. Oppression is defined as: "to subject a person or a people to a harsh or cruel form of domination, to be a source of worry, of stress, or of trouble to somebody, and to hold something in check or put an end to it; to coerce, tyrannize, dominate, repress, subjugate"—the antonym, however, is liberate!

Let me counteract all your oppression and liberate you from being worn out, worn down, or troubled, so that you will no longer feel the opposition, by telling you it is as simple as this: never ***resist*** opposition, never.

Jesus told us this very thing, do you remember? "But I [Jesus] say to you, do not resist an evil person; but whoever slaps you on your right cheek, turn the other to him also. If anyone wants to sue you and take your shirt, let him have your coat also. Whoever forces you to go one mile, go with him two" (Matthew 5:38–40). In other words, we are not only told *not* to *resist* when someone opposes us; our response, He says, is to go along *happily* and go beyond what is asked for or demanded of us.

Yet, instead, when meeting the mountain that stands in our way, we foolishly decide that the way to move it is to push against it. This is ridiculous when you really think about it rationally. The picture on the cover of this book shows us doing this very thing—trying to do something ridiculous. All of us know that there is no way, no amount of time, and no human strength capable of moving any mountain, big or tiny, by pushing against it. Nevertheless, we women often foolishly think that to push against something or someone (like resisting the men or the children in our lives) will get us what we want. We keep doing it, because—at times—we may get what we want. However, as a result, those same men or our children turn a bitter heart against us, and relationships we cherished are ultimately broken.

However, the woman who really "has it all," the one who "gets her cake and eats it too," is a woman who knows *not* to resist, but is terribly *agreeable,* so that men, and all the people around her, *want* to bless her and not oppose her. It is not because they really "want to" do so. It is simply the way God has set up the universe.

Trying to stop power is like trying to put our finger in an electric light socket so that the energy doesn't come out and hurt us. That energy is enough to kill us, and in fact, this is what will happen emotionally each time you try to resist the force of opposition.

Jesus said NOT TO resist evil for good reason: He knew that it was not only foolish, but that it was *contrary* to the laws of the universe. Instead, He and His life teach us the power of **no resistance.**

6. Opposition

Water is the power that proves that the ultimate energy source is that of **nonresistance.** Water *adapts* to all situations, and yet, this power of nonresistance is able to create energy to light a huge city and to create wonders like the Grand Canyon and Niagara Falls. It also can change *your* world magnificently, once you learn to tap into its truth, which is simply—don't resist opposition.

In the midst of writing this book, the Lord has been faithful to put some horrendous mountains in my life in order for me to learn, and therefore to teach you, what it takes to move a mountain. Since you are reading this book, it means, dear one, that He has chosen *you* to begin moving the mountains in your life, in order to get the attention of everyone around you. Who doesn't have mountains that need moving? Then in the process of you moving your mountain, if you follow His plan, soon many will ask you to tell them more, as they watch your mountain begin moving, done so in utter peace and without effort. This, thereby, will give you the opportunity to introduce them to Who has given you the power they are witnessing in your life. This is true evangelism. This is how to "witness" to the unbeliever.

As I said in chapter one, the Lord has you start with the little mountains; then, He will ask you to move a greater one with the same principle. This is what happened to me in the course of a few days. I believe that sharing this story/testimony with you will give you a picture, which is worth a thousand words, so that you will remember how and why.

To keep our family and ministry running, we have no less than four telephone services that I pay for each month. One, in particular, has caused me much frustration for years, which I spoke about briefly in the last chapter. Now, looking back, I see their mistakes (and attitude) were all part of teaching me this very important principle, of nonresistance, to moving mountains.

Overcharges surfaced that the Lord had me put off for weeks and *wait* to take care of. Honestly, I didn't understand why, but since I was so extremely busy, letting it go was not *that* hard to do. Then, something else happened that forced me, at that exact moment in time, to "have to" take care of it. When I contacted them, the Lord reminded me that I must keep a very positive, kind attitude—no matter what. So, I made sure my voice was cheery when I attempted to explain the situation. Everything went surprisingly well, until I asked about the additional charges (just about double what they should have been) for the previous four months, when the representative suddenly turned ugly. Pay attention, because this is the opposition and evil we are *not* to resist, even though we naturally feel that way. We must be like clean, fresh, adapting water allowing ourselves to flow effortlessly, by being so agreeable that it turns the spiritual tide and forces that are trying to come against us.

As the Lord had lovingly taught me throughout my divorce, I *enthusiastically agreed* that the additional money was "no big deal," and I even "thanked" her. Then, immediately, the tide turned when she said, "Can you hang on while I get a supervisor? Maybe he can refund the extra charges," and that is exactly what happened! No effort, no push, it was, it is, the path of no resistance.

Though this was a small mountain moved, the technique and result was significant. It was the way the Lord trained me for the huge feat on the very next day that I also spoke of in the previous chapter, and I will do so again. Even though I am feeling a bit uncomfortable about writing a second chapter about the very same testimony, I will happily *not resist* my own flesh that does not want to appear foolish.

Wow, that's it, isn't it? We're our own worst enemy! From large steps, like writing the identical testimony in two chapters of a book that will be published, to steps as small and insignificant as the hair color I just chose to put on my hair, we are afraid of appearing foolish if we do something wrong, aren't we?!

When I felt the Lord prompting me to use the same testimony (that I actually wrote last week, then wrote again, not realizing I was writing it *again,* until it was almost finished), just a moment later, I got up and went in to see on the counter the hair color that the Lord prompted me to buy, then use. But the impulse to *resist* welled up in me, which now I know, has its source in pride. Wow, I should have known.

6. Opposition 51

Who of us wants to appear the fool? Not me, that's for sure, and not you either. Am I right or am I right? And now that the Lord has uncovered the source of why we resist His promptings, which is simply our pride, it is safe to say that the difficulty of using this testimony was due to my pride—appearing foolish because I wrote about the testimony of getting this miracle honeymoon that my son and his fiancé later rejected. Amazingly revealing, isn't it?

So, what's the solution? Well, for starters, I went ahead and colored my hair with a tone of red that might be too intense, like the last one I felt led to try. Nevertheless, I would rather look foolish than to miss the lesson that is sure to do *more* for my life than what hair color I have on my head! So, to keep moving that mountain I must take the next baby step, yes, to write about the very same testimony—two chapters in a row, because, guess what? When I made the decision in my mind that I would do it no matter how stupid I might appear, the Lord reminded me of how the Bible tells the same story, testimony, or parable over, and over again, doesn't it? And though you might remind me that it is because the stories were written by different people, to show that God was just confirming what Jesus said, my pride was way ahead of you. That reason for resisting already tried, but lost, so here goes.

About three weeks ago, I got a shocking telephone call from my son, of whom I spoke in a testimony in my book *Poverty Mentality*. The Lord had allowed me to bless my son and his fiancé with a honeymoon that (had I paid for it) would have cost *more* than their wedding. It was one of the most amazing and thrilling experiences of my life!

But an emotional tragedy struck, when, just a few weeks before the wedding, my son called one evening simply saying that they had decided not to go, that it wasn't the right time, and he went on to say that things were financially tight. It wasn't just that they weren't going; it was also the fact that they knew that everything would be lost: both the resort and the flights were non-transferable, no refunds, and absolutely no changes. And it wasn't that they didn't know the finality of these reservations—they were right there when I was booking everything, and I was careful, each step of the way, to ask them, when the booking agents asked me, "Are you sure, since nothing can be changed after this point?"

During each portion of booking, the agents asked at least three times and then printed it **boldly** on the confirmation sheet, so that they had to know all would be lost if they backed out.

Since their lack of finances was said to be one of the reasons, I immediately told him that I was more than happy to give them enough money to cover *everything,* in order to save the already invested points and flying miles that I would lose if they bailed out. But it was clear that *this* was not the real reason, and none was really ever revealed. Honestly, it hit me hard, harder than I would have imaged, so I went to my prayer closet for comfort and understanding. I was honestly devastated.

After many tears, the Lord simply said, "Michele, can you trust me?" and of course, I could.

Being discreet was my main concern at this point. I knew that if my other children heard about this, they would struggle with unkind feelings toward the couple, and I didn't want that. But God had other ideas, because just hours later the other children heard it from their own mouths, when their brother and his fiancé came over to try to make everyone understand. From that day on, this atrocity had been spread around to just about everyone we knew, despite my efforts to keep it silent—but I had to know that this, too, was all a part of God's plan. How would He turn it for good? The awesomeness of it all is that we never need to know HOW; we simply just have to KNOW that HE will.

It began to turn on the day the news reached my older son, who told his fiancé, and they set out to "try to do something," maybe take the "vacation" themselves with another couple—anything, they said, to ease the blow to me. Isn't that just too sweet?! However, none of their efforts proved to do anything, except to prove that this mountain was immovable. And then…

6. Opposition

Signs that this mountain just may move began to surface. First, my other son's fiancé told him that if the tickets and reservations could be changed, she would marry him *immediately* and use it as their honeymoon (something she would never consider when he hinted about this kind of a wedding; when she couldn't find a place to have their wedding, or find the dress, or where to hold their reception). Next, she told her mother about the situation, who said, "Darling, if the arrangements work out—go for it! This is God, no doubt!!" This statement was from a mother who had told her daughter, since she was a little girl, that if she ever ran off to marry without her being there, she would disown her!

Next, they, too, spoke of not having any money, when all of a sudden, my son's fiancé remembered that her mother had given her the money for their wedding ahead of time. Signs that the mountain just *might* move were emerging everywhere! That's when I saw the mountain begin to quiver, just a bit, and I began to get excited at the thought of what I believed was about to happen.

The next significant move was when my son's fiancé called me one morning, telling me that she so wanted to pursue this dream, but that my son had said that they shouldn't. She told me that she didn't want to go against his authority, since he was her spiritual leader, so what should she do? Oh, my, did I feel blessed. Wow. That's when I was given the opportunity (as an older woman who was sought for guidance) to share with her that as a woman, especially as a wife, when situations come up like this, when we feel something strongly, that we shouldn't talk about it to anyone, but instead, as Mary did, "ponder it in your heart." If it were God's plan, her fiancé would have a change of heart.

Just about an hour later, my son called and told me that he could tell this was something his fiancé really wanted, so, what could he do to make it happen? Thank You, Lord!! God turned his heart when he saw her quietly submit, and when I was wise enough to also keep silent and watch the miracle unfold. Because as a mother it is tempting to speak to our children who are grown, nevertheless, who better to speak to than our own HH who so wonderful waits and even longs to take care of things for us, and to do it so beautifully without a ripple or consequence. So, now, since my son came out and *asked* me what he could do, I told him that the two of us needed to look at what we COULD do rather than trying to do what we couldn't.

This was the lesson the Lord had showed me two months in a row, when He prompted me to do my own taxes, which, here I go again, I spoke about in a previous chapter. Again, I saw that this was another reason why He led me to do my taxes; He needed to build my faith in impossibilities *and* to teach me this principle: When you know that God wants you to move a mountain, look at what you CAN do, rather than what you can't.

Again, I asked my son, "What *can* **you** do?" and what came to mind was to ask him "If this works, *where* are you getting married?" He told me "There! In Hawaii—I believe we should have a destination wedding!" Then I asked him if he knew if there was a waiting period in that state, and he wasn't sure. So, he set out to research the details. *To understand how much of an "impossibility" this miracle was, this conversation occurred on Monday afternoon, and the flight for Hawaii was scheduled for early Saturday morning.

Then I sought the Lord for what I *could* do. Immediately, He brought the honeymoon folder to mind, the one that I had never given my other son, which stood as another sign to me. Since I still had it, this was the Lord's plan all along. There were signs popping up everywhere that were clear: why this couple could never find a place to have their wedding, could never find the right dress, didn't hear from the church that wanted to hire my son–it all made sense now. God had another plan for this couple, which led to increase my faith that this was going to happen!

The Lord led me to look in the folder and to see that there were three parts to this mountain, and the next step was to move the second most impossible part—the resort. Again, it was non-transferable, but I just knew that nothing was impossible with God, and if this were indeed His plan, it would happen. It took all of five minutes on the phone—done! Again, amazing and impossible. This, too, served to strengthen our faith (my son's, his fiancé, and mine) to believe God for it all.

Honestly, the rental car never really posed a concern to me, since to forfeit it would not be a huge financial loss; however, even this was accomplished supernaturally when the Lord led me to cancel it (which by the way I had tried unsuccessfully with this same site on one of my own trips). Yet, this time I cancelled without penalty, then, when I asked out loud, "What should I do now Lord?" I saw in big, bold, red letters "Do you want to reserve another car?" I just laughed, and said "Yes," and clicked!

Two down, now just one to go! Of course, the last part was the hardest. At least it was what *we* deemed the hardest—all feats are equally the same for God. As I told my son and his fiancé, "All our difficulties and His miracles are the same to Him; He is not sitting up there thinking, 'Oh, my, now let Me think how I am going to do this one.'" We just knew that we could all see, and now believed, that it was His will, and that, of course, nothing was impossible for God—the mountain was about to move!

The next step to moving this mountain was when I got a call that my son was in line at the airport to speak to them directly about making the transfer. His fiancé called to tell me to "pray." She said that her spiritual mother whom she had told earlier that day (who began to cry and to have Goosebumps when she heard the details) had told her own husband, who flies a lot, to tell my son to *go* to the airport, that when they saw him, they would make the changes. That's when the Lord reminded me of something I had seen, a vision, of my son in line at the airport a few days earlier, so just before I hung up, I shared this with my son's fiancé to encourage her that "this was it!"

Excitedly, I went into the living room to speak to the Lord (as she had asked) with my youngest three children (all who have faith like a child), and we began to rejoice that it was about to happen. I just knew, that I knew, that I knew that it was going to happen in an instant; therefore, I began to act as if it had already happened!

About an hour later, I got a call from my son—he was on his way home, and he told me that the airline had tried and tried, but the fields on the computer screen that needed to be opened to make the right changes would not come up. The ticketing agent at the airport said that the only person who could make these kinds of changes was the booking agent where I redeemed my flying miles. Though my feelings wanted to plummet, and so did his, I told him that this was simply "the next step." I hung up and made the call, only to find out that they had closed. We had missed them by only ten minutes.

Still, I told my son that it was all part of His plan, that God needed to show me something, and that's when He led me to the fine print on a document, online, that said in bold letters, that the tickets were non-transferable, no changes, etc. etc. But then... it went on to say, deep within the paragraph in tiny, tiny small print, that if the airline did approve a change, we were to contact them *first!* There it was, "it was written," now all I had to do was wait until morning to contact them *first!!*

Again, this delay only proved that the Lord needed to show me something else, or maybe just that I needed to speak to someone who would be working the following morning, or like discussed in the last chapter, the wait served to renew my spiritual strength that I'd need for the last baby step. For whatever reason, it was all part of His plan! That night I fell asleep quickly, but I woke abruptly at 4 A.M. Not only were those four hours (while I waited for the office to open) not wasted, but they also proved to build my excitement and expectation, as the Lord led me to finish rewriting earlier chapters of this book. As I read and rewrote, it proved to build my faith in His ability and desire to move this mountain as I spoke!

Watching the last three minutes click by, I was trembling with excitement. (Mind you, the excitement wanted to appear as fear, which we will discuss in more detail in chapter 9). When I finally placed the call, the Lord reminded me of the way of **no resistance** and *cheerfulness* that had worked so miraculously the day before with the telephone company *when* they had opposed me.

Sure enough, the first person I spoke to assured me with determined opposition that what I wanted to do was impossible—then, would you believe, she proceeded to sell me something? This is when our emotions want to jump out of our skin (and out our mouths)—that's the challenge, isn't it? It is challenging to continue to stay peaceful, most of all, agreeable, and not let haste or hurry, which leads to panic, take over. And so, I quietly listened to her sales speech, even excitedly, but then was able to kindly tell her I had just purchased what she wanted to sell me, but I thanked her profusely, which led her to say, "Hey, now, wait a minute, let me see if they might be able to help you in this department," and she transferred me.

Without going through each of the next seven people I talked to, the final step was when I spoke to a woman in charge of redeeming flying miles, who assured me that the airline **did** have the power to change the details of the flight, even though they said they didn't, and she gave me the airline telephone number to try.

Throughout this whole ordeal I was told the same thing: that the points would have to be refunded, then new tickets would have to be booked and re-ticketed from scratch, which by this late date, would surely be an entirely new mission impossible.

Yet, "nothing is impossible with God"—that's what I read years ago, when I read Erin's testimony. When I read it, I told the Lord that if He did the impossible by restoring my marriage after adultery and divorce, just like He did for Erin, since I, too, had a husband who said he would never come back to me because he didn't love me and never did—then I would join Erin to tell the world that nothing was impossible for Him. God did restore the impossible, and has since seen fit to keep more impossibilities coming into my life to continue to prove this is principle is TRUE and to join forces with Erin.

In an instant, I heard the lady on the phone, whose name was Deborah (remember in the Bible that Deborah was a prophetess who was a judge in Israel who led the army for Barak?). Well, it was Deborah who told me to "hold" while she CHANGED THE NAMES! What? We had been told since 9/11 that it was illegal to change names on airline tickets. With rapt anticipation, I sat on "hold" for more than 20 minutes for our miracle to become reality. But, ever so kindly, every few minutes she came on to thank me for my patience, because this is just something that they NEVER did, so they really didn't know how to do it! It was after the second time she reassured me that tears welled up in my eyes because I was really watching my mountain, the one that had caused me so much pain, fall into the sea! The emotions were more than I could hold back now, and I began to weep in abandoned joy.

Then, right after she came back the third time, when she told me that they were "almost done," I leaped up out of my chair to praise the Lord and pulled my back out, completely. Ouch. All I could do was laugh—and to sit back down in pain, but my heart was soaring.

When she thanked me and we hung up I was stunned, crying, and shaking, as I tried to contact my son. While screaming I told him, which woke my children up, so as I spoke to my son, my children were right there dancing around—their brother was getting married in Hawaii!! Oh, how romantic—and even more, God had moved a mountain of impossible proportion! **The End, again.**

*Well, then, there you have it. Now, can I ask you something; be honest: Were you one of the ones who read the testimony through, again, or did you skip down to the bottom of the page? Just asking, because I completely understand those of you who were a bit bored with hearing this testimony a second time.

While reading this through, after I refused to continue to resist writing this same, exact testimony in my book, so many things tried to oppose me. The first I was just reminded of when I wrote "exact" testimony. While going over it again (as I usually do when I write), I kept wondering if what I wrote was "exact" and it made me want to go back to the previous chapter to check.

You understand; what if I wrote something a bit *differently?* I would lose credibility with my readers, wouldn't I? Once again, this stronghold of pride is quite determined to hold on, isn't it? However, as I continued to do what the Lord was leading me to do, and doing my best not to resist His leading (all while doing my best to oppose my own pride), I was reminded of a couple of reasons *why* He might have led me to do this small, but very revealing task.

6. Opposition 59

Two of the most life-changing testimonies I had to hear at least *twice* for it to take hold of me. And both times, would you believe it, I thought to myself, "Why is he telling this same story?" and my opinion of these two men dropped, just a bit.

Years before, when a visiting evangelist began to tell the same story, I wondered just how he could go around to different churches and tell the same story over and over again: Didn't he take notes so he didn't repeat himself, or was it because his life was so shallow that this was all he had to offer? What a stinker I am! Funny thing is, there are more than a few of you who thought the same thing about me—now be honest! Yet, I know that had I not heard the same exact story of the little girl who was dying, who said simply, "Don't worry about me, I have **all I want and all I need,** *I have **Jesus***" I would never have experienced the abundant life I am now living. And speaking of living...

Had I not heard the story my pastor told about the man who cried out to God "out loud" when he was held at gunpoint, not caring who heard his cry, I would not have done the very same thing when my husband (at the time) and I were the first to see two boys in a ditch after, what should have been, a fatal car accident. With that story fresh in my mind (since he told it over and over again—at least *three* times), I, too, cried out to God, very loudly in front of the crowd that stood around me. I cried out in a loud voice in order to save that boy who laid there, and did it again moments later when I could see he was about to die (as blood filled his lungs and he was fighting to breath). Both times God moved, the second instantly brought a man who did a tracheotomy right there in the ditch with my son's knife and a dusting cloth that I had just used to wipe down our car's dashboard!

That boy's life might have been spared due in part to my pastor who chose to share the same story over and over again, which was too many times, in my opinion. Now my opinion has changed. Could it be that both these men shared the same story, the same testimony for *my* benefit, and not because they stupidly forgot it was a repeat, or because they had nothing better to share? Could it just be that they resisted their pride in order to change my life and to save a young man's life?

"Do not judge according to appearance, but judge with righteous judgment" (John 7:24).

"I can do nothing on My own initiative As I hear, I judge; and My judgment is just, because I do not seek My own will, but the will of Him who sent Me" (John 5:30).

"Therefore let us not judge one another anymore, but rather determine this—not to put an obstacle or a stumbling block in a brother's way" (Romans 14:13).

"But if we judged ourselves rightly, we would not be judged" (1 Corinthians 11:31).

*Years later I heard the young man lived and his family had tried to find and thank me for openly crying out the Lord. They were Christians and God has used this young man, who lived but was instantly paralyzed, in many ways as he became a motivational speaker.

Chapter 7

Simply Speak

"You will **say** to this mountain,
'Move from here to there,' and it will move;
And **nothing** will be impossible to you."
—Matthew 17:20

There is no principle more important than having control over what you speak. "You will *say to this **mountain**, 'Move from here to there,' and it will move;* and nothing will be impossible to you" (Matthew 17:20).

Most people, Christian or not, haven't any idea of the creative power of our words. Even though I had read and studied endlessly two of Erin's books that devote two entire chapters in each, four chapters to learn that we should be careful what we say in our marriage (or other relationships we hold dear to our hearts.) Yet, until now, I had no idea how truly powerful our words can be in determining what we attract, when we react, resulting in a positive or a negative outcome.

It wasn't until just recently that I began to wonder if my marriage restoration was due more to what I believed, and as a result, **said,** than it was by my following the seemingly endless list of other principles laid out in the two books I wore out reading. Was it more what I said, than what I did? I began to wonder.

Again, speaking stems from what we have hidden *within* our hearts, which is what we believe, and is primarily because of what we can imagine. So just to *say* something, without feeling it, is not what will move a mountain; only those things that you truly believe in your heart will result in you feeling it and speaking it out loud with the power of moving impossible obstacles. (We will discuss the importance of our feelings in chapter 9.)

Not only is what you speak the most powerful principle to moving mountains, in a way, it is also the principle that is the most fun when you understand its power.

It really caught my attention just a few months ago, when the Lord began to reveal to me a secret that I already *basically* knew, which is: Since we are all created in the image of God, we also hold the power of creating our world: good and bad. God simply *spoke* the world into existence—*simply spoke.* Then later, we see Jesus doing the very same thing: he *simply spoke* to calm the sea and the wind; He also *spoke* and told Lazarus to come forth, thereby raising him from the dead.

We have to pay close attention to how Jesus moved mountains, because when He was about to go to the cross, He told His disciples, His followers (you and me), that **we** would be able to do far greater feats than what we had seen Him do. But are we? No. This means that we are not utilizing the power that He died to give us, mainly because we are ignorant of that power and misuse it horribly.

While talking to my dear, sweet neighbor, I was telling her about the book that I was writing at that time, *The Poverty Mentality,* which deals more with *how we **think**,* good and bad, which led to *how we will **speak*** about it, since how we speak, good and bad, is implanted in our hearts. There are no less than twenty-seven times in the Bible where speaking is linked to our heart: did you know that? Here's just one of my favorites:

"The good man out of the good treasure of his heart brings forth what is good; and the evil man out of the evil treasure brings forth what is evil; for his mouth speaks from that which fills his heart" (Luke 6:45).

That was when my neighbor told me about a new video and book that revealed a *secret,* and the movie shows that the principle originated from a very old book—a book that is never revealed in this video. The interesting thing is, when she told me about it, I instantly knew I had the book—it was sitting next to my bed, a gift that had been given to me by a fellowship member I met while in Colorado on my *very first* travel destination, during the same month as my divorce. Interesting. What's most interesting, like other methods that "work," is that the principle is really from the Bible.

The book confirmed to me, when I read it (then and just recently), that the power of how we think, which leads to what we believe, which turns the heart, would naturally cause us to have peace or joy as we speak of what we think about—it all began to come together beautifully. It was then, at that moment, that I knew that I would have to write this book *Moving Mountains*. All the principles to move those foreboding mountains in our lives were out there just waiting to be corralled into a book, which would unleash the joy that the abundant life held for every woman who wanted **all** that Jesus died to give her.

Though these "secret" principles work for non-Christians, and even when a person removes God from the picture (which is what this video and the book carefully chooses to do), it does **not** make it unscriptural or prove it is unsafe for the Christian to believe or act upon. To believe this would mean that we are ignorant of what Jesus Himself said in Matthew 5:45, "For He causes His sun to rise on the **evil** and the **good**, and sends **rain** on the righteous and the unrighteous." God is a God who blesses anyone, whenever anyone follows the laws God created, correct? For instance, if someone respects gravity, or chooses to ignore it, that has nothing to do with whether or not he or she is a Christian, right? There was a whole movement not too long ago about the "power of positive thinking" which worked, of course, because it's one of God's laws.

In addition, this principle of the power of what we speak is literally *everywhere* in the Bible. Yet, even though it is right under our very noses, day after day, as we read our Bibles for our morning devotionals, we forget what we read, and we walk right out into our day violating His principles, one after another. And I am not talking about sin; I am simply talking about how we are robbed, day after day, of what Jesus shed His blood for: Allowing us to live a life of abundance, rather than struggling with lack. "The thief comes only to steal and kill and destroy; I came that they may have **life**, and have it *abundantly"* (John 10:10).

As I have done with just about every chapter of this book, I want to share with you a few stories that will help you to understand more fully that you need to pay close attention to *what you say*. "Now therefore, my sons, listen to me, and **pay attention** to the words of my mouth" (Proverbs 7:24). For in our words are the "power of life or death," "**Death** and **life** are in the **power** of the tongue, and those who love it will eat its fruit" (Proverbs 18:21).

Whether you experience joy or sorrow, abundance or lack, will usually be contained within your words; will you choose to learn and finally live this truth? Since the Bible tells us that many "will die for **lack** of instruction, and in the greatness of his folly he will go astray" (Proverbs 5:23).

Why is it important? So "the ransomed of the LORD will return and come with **joyful** shouting to Zion, with everlasting **joy** upon their heads they will find gladness and **joy**, and **sorrow** and sighing will flee away" (Isaiah 35:10).

Just read these next verses from Isaiah 55, with which many of you are familiar, but this time, with what this chapter has taught you so far:

"'Ho! Every one who thirsts, come to the waters; and you who have no money come, buy and eat. Come, buy wine and milk without money and without cost. Why do you spend money for what is not bread, and your wages for what does not satisfy? Listen carefully to Me, and eat what is good, and *delight yourself in **abundance***. Incline your ear and come to Me. Listen, that you may live; and I will make an everlasting covenant with you, according to the faithful mercies shown to David...

"'For My thoughts are not your thoughts, nor are your ways My ways,' declares the LORD. For as the heavens are higher than the earth, so are My ways higher than your ways and My thoughts than your thoughts...

7. Simply Speak

"'So will My word be which goes forth from My mouth; It will not return to Me empty, without accomplishing what I desire, and without succeeding in the matter for which I sent it. For you will go out with joy and be led forth with peace; the *mountains* and the *hills* will *break forth* into shouts of **joy** before you.'" (Isaiah 55:1-3, 8-9, 11-12)

The new revelation of the power of what we simply speak began to unfold when my son decided that he needed to have steady income to "*just* make his car payment." Please notice the word I bolded and italicized. "*Just*" —so simple a word yet it holds so much power. Since he asked, God opened the door for a job that he worked terribly hard at, but he made "just" enough to meet his car payment. He was hoping to make a lot in tips, which he should have gotten, since he is a hard worker, has lots of personality, and has a handsome look to complement these other traits. However, what he asked for was to "*just* make his car payment." That's what I told him when he came home very late one night and asked me what I thought was wrong. I explained that God gave him *just* what he had asked for, "just." Because he was exhausted after working a double shift, and so terribly frustrated, he then said, "Okay then, if it's what I speak, let me say this! 'I want a job where I can use my God-given talents, doing what I really *enjoy* doing. I want some great paying jobs in media, doing camera work!!'"

Most of you might question the validity of what I am going to say, but the truth is: within a week, my son received a call from a guy who wanted him to manage the camera work for his team (similar to putting together a union) for production companies that come to this area from Hollywood. These film companies would rather use local film crews, instead of flying in their own production team and equipment. What my son began making *per day* was MORE than what he would have made working **double** *shifts as a waiter for an entire* **month***!*

*This is the same power that God gave each of us, but unfortunately, we ignorantly speak *against* ourselves rather than *for* ourselves.

A short time later, my son was talking to me about his brother, who had been offered a position as a Media Director but wasn't sure if he wanted it. My son, who is primarily a cameraman, said that a Media Director's job was exactly what he wanted some day. So, together we spoke about it, and he said that he didn't have the training that his brother did, and he needed more in the area of directing.

Would you believe that just a few *days* later, one evening, my son was running out the door to TD at a local church (technical director, who is the person who pushes the buttons for the director, just one position away from the director). While he was running out the door, I smiled and said, "Next, God will have you Direct!" which happened that very evening! Two-thirds of the way through the church service, the director pushed his seat back and told my son to take over—my son directed the remainder of the service!

Have I caught your attention yet? If not, now listen to this. It was about ten days later that I walked by my son, who was on the couch talking to a young man who I didn't recognize (but that happens all the time). The next morning, my son asked me if I knew who he was, and why he was there, and what he was talking to him about. When I said no, he went on to tell me that this young man's father was the pastor of a mega church in San Diego, and he wanted my son to be its Media Director!

My son and I spoke it, and there it was manifested right before our eyes, and well before my son felt he was even ready. What he spoke, saying what he wanted, came to him. Even now it is pending, as is the position for his brother. Even though they both readily know this principle, and it's been reinforced by what they've witnessed me doing, I still see that so often they ignore its power and often speak that they are "not sure if they want it" (the positions). So, the positions remain pending.

How many of you are getting this? What we speak is powerful. Whether or not we say things consistently, not just if we say positive versus negative things.

7. Simply Speak 67

Not convinced? Let me go on. After the recent car accident that my daughter had, I drove her to and from work, while her car was being repaired. I began to dread these times, because my daughter has been extremely negative, ever since her dad left her. (That's how our children feel, you know; even though your husband might have walked out on you, your children, especially your daughters, were rejected by him, and they feel it immensely.) Normally I just listen, since to say something only brings about a more negative reaction; I know you understand what I mean.

On this particular morning, I lovingly interrupted her with a very positive and powerful tone of voice. I asked her *why* she kept talking about her job with all its problems. Didn't she know that it kept unleashing more and more negative things in her life? She didn't like me interrupting her, nor what I'd said, but then I turned our conversation toward a positive note and related the recent events in her brother's life that I just shared with you. She knew all about them, but she had not looked at the chain of events all at the same time. It got her attention, and she immediately said, "Well, okay, then what I really want is a job at the church [naming it] and for it to pay well, so that I can quit my job here!" Then she said that she would go over and fill out an application.

Unfortunately, I needed to break in again, because I felt the prompting of her Father, my HH, saying that she had so many connections (she has volunteered in so many areas of the church for almost 7 years), and I sensed she should simply talk to one of the pastors she knew and worked with. When I began naming them, she jumped on the second name, Pastor Brandon.

It was about 7 A.M. when she said that, and just hours later, at 2 P.M., while I was in the chiropractor's office, I heard someone call my name, and when I turned around to see "who" was speaking—of course, it was Pastor Brandon! I laughed, since I had not seen or spoken to him in almost a year, but there he was for me to tell him that my daughter was hoping for a job at the church and needed his advice.

The job didn't end up coming through him, but through God and in yet another divine appointment. This is another principle that you need to know, never fixate yourself on someone or something. Just simply move as your HH continues to lead you. Too many people miss this and wonder why they never move forward. It is not the person, nor the situation—it is simply God who will move you as you continue to believe and to speak positively and refrain from the negative. In addition, we have already discussed timing, correct? As it says in Habakkuk 2:2-3, everything is set for an appointed time. "Then the LORD answered me and said, 'Record the vision and inscribe it on tablets, that the one who reads it may run. For the vision is yet for the appointed time; it hastens toward the goal and it will not fail. Though it tarries, WAIT for it; for it will certainly come, it will not delay.'"

The more you absorb the truth in this principle the more you'll realized that some connections take longer, so we must be willing to wait, if it is necessary, to catch the next flow of events. (Picture how we connect in a train station or an airline flight while traveling.) Also, add to this what we learned in prior chapters, that often He knows we need more spiritual strength then we have, so it means we need to wait in order to "renew our strength."

Your life can be like this; it really can. It only takes *tuning in* to what is constantly happening in your life as you speak. Until now, you were simply unaware of it. And another secret to this principle of the creative power of what you speak is that you and I will be able to see it in other people's lives much more clearly than you and I can see it in our own lives. So, to fine-tune this principle in your mind, you, too, should become a sort of "Moving Mountain Coach" for those to whom you are closest. It will result in you being much more aware of what you speak, when you help others realize the power they possess, since they, too, are made in the image of God and were in our Savior's mind when He chose to walk the road to the cross on Calvary.

*Just remember, if you live it, others will witness it, and soon they will ask. Until then, be quiet and live it—until asked.

Now, back to the story. The divine appointments (or coincidences as many people want to call them) didn't stop with speaking to the pastor. The very next day, I picked up my daughter to bring her to the bank with a copy of her insurance, but she had forgotten to print it. Right now, I can't remember why I had my laptop in the car, but I did, so we headed over to church, rather than going back home, because they had Wi-Fi.

Here is another principle that I am keenly aware of that I need to share: God sets us up to do things that are unusual, and even to forget something on purpose—it's all part of His plan. And when you sense you should do something, like me grabbing my computer, do not stop to reason! With what you've learned, read Proverbs 3:5–6 to see how so many get off course, "Trust in the Lord with all your heart and do not *lean* on your own understanding. In all your ways acknowledge Him, and He will make your paths straight." When you *lean* to your understanding, like I could have done when grabbing my laptop, "What do I need this for? Why put it in the car when it's safer at home?"—the flow would have been broken.

To live abundantly, we must stop running around ignorant of what is happening. We really need to, again, tune in to this incredible world, each day, that the Lord makes for us, equipped with all the principles that make up this abundant life!

As soon as my daughter said that we should run to the church, I could literally "feel" that something was about to happen. Once you begin to become aware of the spiritual realm that we are a part of every day of our lives, you, too, will soon be able to *sense* when a miracle or spiritual blessing is about to happen.

As we walked in, I just kept looking around, wondering where this miracle or blessing was about to come from. After a few minutes, I had to just give the whole thing to the Lord, since I thought I might be wrong or that I was trying to make something happen. I didn't want to get into the flesh, pushing against that mountain, when all that God asks us to do is to simply speak and to tell it to move.

A moment later, I spotted a Starbucks kiosk, and I asked my daughter if she wanted anything. She said no, but I kept on asking her. Then I stood up and told her that I was going to get something. Now, let me see if I can explain this. I normally would never ask someone something twice, as I did with my daughter. In addition, I never, ever drink coffee, after my first cup in the morning. Never. The flavor doesn't appeal to me. Nevertheless, there I was at the counter.

Then it was like my eyes were opened, and I asked the lady there if she was hiring. She looked at me kind of funny. Maybe she thought I was too old to work there or not the type who would work making coffee at Starbucks. But the real reason she looked at me like that, stunned, was because she had just hung up the phone, after speaking to a girl who she had let go (on the phone), because she had not shown up for work that day! And at that very moment, the Lord had led us to walk in. Coincidence? Or, was this indeed a divine appointment, due to what we both believed and spoke about? "Again I say to you, that if **two of you agree** on earth about anything that they may ask, it shall be done for them by My Father Who is in heaven" (Matthew 18:19).

That's when I pointed to my daughter who was on my laptop, as I began telling the lady at the Starbucks counter that *she* wanted a job, working **at** the church. We spoke some more, then I took my coffee over and told my daughter about what had just happened, telling her to go over and talk to her. She simply said, "No, thank you," and we left. As I said, for the past two years, since her dad left her, she has resisted everyone and everything and has become primarily negative about life.

Nevertheless, you know what? I didn't oppose her. You see, you and I have to follow *all* the principles. And we learned in the last chapter that we are not to resist or oppose when a negative or a counter power comes against us. So, I didn't. God and His power of goodness are greater than any negative power that exists. Our outcome only depends on where we plug ourselves into: negative or positive force.

Yet, within 48 hours, my daughter called me from the Starbucks kiosk to tell me that she had gotten the job! And you will never believe just how she got it. The manager was speaking to the wife of the senior pastor (not the Pastor Brandon) telling her she needed to hire someone, when she said, "I know who you should hire!" and the pastor's wife said my daughter's name. The manager was shocked because that morning my daughter had gone back in and filled out an application, unbeknownst to me. No one told the pastor's wife, nor had she just seen her either time my daughter was there at the church. Yes, my daughter had been a close friend with her daughter years ago, before her daughter went off to college. The only explanation was that what we speak, due to what we believe, as a result of what we choose to imagine, is a force that is more powerful and more at work in our lives—much more than what we realize.

Each and every day, I see the results of what I speak and what is spoken about in the lives of those around me. Try it yourself, study the Scriptures, and you will see for yourself that what we simply speak about will happen, even to the extent of moving a mountain.

Chapter 8

Final Hurdle?

"Because you're not yet taking God seriously"
—Matthew 17:20 MSG

Why hasn't my life changed? Why haven't the promises I know God gave me come to pass? I think it's "'Because you're not yet taking God seriously,' said Jesus. 'The simple truth is that if you had a mere kernel of faith, a poppy seed, say, you would tell this mountain, 'Move!' and it would move. There is nothing you wouldn't be able to tackle'" (Matthew 17:20 MSG). That's what Jesus said to us.

Has God indeed given us the keys, but have we failed to properly use them, just because we haven't taken Him seriously? "I will give you the **keys** of the kingdom of **heaven**; and whatever you bind on earth shall have been bound in **heaven**, and whatever you loose on earth shall have been loosed in **heaven**" (Matthew 16:19). What have you "loosed" into your life, and what have you bound—not in some wild, loud prayer, but in a way that will move mountains, by simply speaking it, the same way Jesus did?

Are happiness and prosperity, the abundant life Jesus died to give you, reigning free in your life? Or have you, instead, loosed doom, gloom, fear and failure?

The final hurdle, I believe, is when you and I really and completely walk around, speak about and meditate on what we *believe* about our situation. Speak to and about our mountain in a manner that will unleash the power that God gave us to cast it into the sea—setting us free to receive His blessings on our lives. We need to "Heal the sick, raise the dead, cleanse the lepers, cast out demons. **Freely** you *received,* **freely** *give*" (Matthew 10:8). "Now we have *received*, not the spirit of the world, but the Spirit who is from God, so that we may know the things **freely** given to us by God" (1 Corinthians 2:12).

The power to move mountains, just like salvation or the baptism of the Holy Spirit, is not something that we need to earn. God gave. Being free from debt, pain, worry and sin are all the same to God. None is less achievable *with* Him, and therefore it is simply offered to us without any of our effort or costing us anything. Who does God include in this offer? Why, *"you* who have no money **come, buy** and eat. **Come, buy**...*without money* and *without cost"* (Isaiah 55:1). Will your doubt and fear cause you to stumble over what I believe may be the "final" hurdle, as happened with me?

I believe that my final hurdle may also be the most important, because the finish line is finally in sight. However, our final hurdle often is the most difficult, because, for one thing, we are tired. My final hurdle came against me with brute force and unexpectedly, pulling out all the stops and boundaries that I believed protected me.

Let me ask you something: Will what you and I *naturally* see and feel cause us to imagine, believe and speak doom, gloom and discouragement? Or will you and I, instead, see that mountain *supernaturally*—based entirely on His promises and on the baby steps we have already faithfully taken? The choice is ours. Did you notice that I include myself in this question? I did, because I believe I had seen that my mountain of debt was showing signs of falling, and I want my feelings, now and forever, to reflect my beliefs, rather than the foreboding spirit that is trying to take hold of me.

In this chapter I will attempt to share my final hurdle; the question is what form will yours take?

Final?

One after another, the mountains were falling left and right, large and small, and then...out of nowhere, I get a huge, thick envelope—a letter from my ex-husband disguised as if he'd sent a check. The check was actually for my daughter, a reimbursement to me for her car's tires. "It's a check," my youngest daughter said, when she happily handed me the envelope. Did you know that the enemy will gain access to your mind, soul, body and spirit in ways, and when, and from whom you least expect? I knew that, and yet I was relaxed and not really *sober* in my thinking, due mainly to the fact that recent events had meant that we (my ex-husband, his new wife, and her children) as a group, were getting along famously. Recently, I had even entertained them in my home, not once, but twice, due to the wedding of my son.

"So then let us not sleep as others do, but let us be alert and **sober**" (1 Thessalonians 5:6). "Be of **sober** spirit, be **on the alert**. Your adversary, the devil, *prowls* around like a roaring lion, seeking someone to devour" (1Peter 5:8). Devour me, he did.

Without thinking, I began to read a horribly vile, condemning letter, loaded with accusations and terrifying threats. Before I knew what had hit me, I heard the Lord tell me to **stop** reading it, which I did, but not soon enough—what I'd read had already taken hold and crushed my heart. That night, I tossed and turned, praying without ceasing, asking God for the whys and hows, to know how to answer it. All the while, I was begging Him to allow me to not have to answer, but instead I was seeking a way to, again, bless my enemy.

Let me veer off for a moment and confess something to you. My flesh wants to take this chapter out of the book. If I'm being honest, my greatest concern, even more than the possibility that I will lose your respect, is that the principle I'm sharing will be misused: used to feed the flesh of those who harbor anger and would love, more than anything, to have a reason, an excuse really, to abuse the principle. And yet, my audience (you dear reader), I believe you to be of the true nature of His bride. Therefore, as His bride, His love has changed your very nature into one of peace, gentleness, goodness and loving those who mistreat you.

Now, back to the hurdle. All in all, this new battle coming against me raged on for more than a week, mostly due to a battle plan that I was not accustomed to, nor familiar with, and that, therefore, I was more than hesitant to take. Prior to this fateful day, I had come to know, embrace and live a life of non-resistance, agreeing with and blessing my enemies. So, as you will certainly be able to imagine, when the Lord had me respond to what was said in complete honesty, yet boldly and, to my shock, in a way that was cynical and at times sarcastic, I questioned my walk with God, my ability to hear Him correctly, and, in many ways, I panicked and felt as if my world was spinning out of control.

Throughout this ordeal, I began asking God "for a word," something that I haven't needed for years. I knew His promises, His ways, His methods and His principles—to the point that the ways of God were hidden deep in my heart, so His Word was always there to guide me. But what do you and I do, when what we sense He is telling us, what we *know* He is telling us, is contrary to all that is peaceful? Our world shakes, quivers, and it shows up in our bodies, minds and spirits.

Yet, God continues to be faithful, unshaken, once again proving, as He said, that "'My thoughts are not your thoughts, neither are your ways My ways,' declares the Lord. 'As the heavens are higher than the earth, so are My ways higher than your ways and My thoughts than your thoughts'" (Isaiah 55:8–9 NIV). Though I didn't understand, and certainly didn't want to, I obeyed.

When I finished responding to the first, long, horrible letter, I let my email sit in my email drafts, not wanting to send it. I desperately needed a sign, a word, and I frantically wanted to know, to understand, why. So, I ventured into my prayer closet, a place I rarely *have to* visit any more. Long gone were the days when I needed to go there in order to hear His still, small voice; it had been almost two years, since I found that I could hear Him anywhere and everywhere. Yet, when confusion enters the mind, it penetrates the soul, and the spiritual connection experiences interference, largely due to fear.

While seeking Him in my prayer closet, rather than giving me answers to my questions, the Lord simply asked me, "Michele, why don't you want to send the email?" My answer was simple, and it caught me off-guard. It was because I was afraid. I was afraid that if I didn't simply "agree" to what my ex-husband had said, and agree to his threatening terms, he would seek revenge. To which He asked me, "And what happens when we base what we do on fear?" My answer again was simple, "Our decision is always wrong."

The Lord continued to ask me why else I didn't want to send it, and that was because I was worried what people would think of me—people like my ex-husband, his wife, my children, and even you, my readers, along with all the RMI's followers. Yes, He showed me that rather than focusing on what **He** thought of me, I had turned my attention to what others would think—again, a mistake.

Coming out of my prayer closet, and now focused on His plan (that made no sense to me), I sent the email.

It took about two days to get the reply I dreaded. My whole being, once again, wanted to run and hide, finding a way of escape, simply because I was not doing what I had done before—I wanted to bless; I wanted to agree; I wanted to go with the flow. "I mean, dear Lord, hadn't I just written about this very principle of non-resistance in the chapter that was just posted on RMI's website?" Again, I fought the thoughts of what everyone would think, knowing deep down in the recesses of my heart that what mattered is what HE *alone* thought of me, and to resist Him was worse than resisting this vile evil that kept coming at me.

Throughout this entire battle (that I believe had to be my final hurdle), the Lord was patient and kept giving me a word, here and there, as I asked Him. When I asked God *why* I was no longer responding in peace and agreement (but only after I'd obeyed and sent the response), I was surprised to read in the little devotional *God Calling* (that I keep in my prayer closet) this...

"Listen, listen, I am your Lord. Before Me there is none other. Just trust me in everything. Help is here all the time. The difficult way is nearly over, but you have learnt it in lessons you could learn in no other way.

"The Kingdom of heaven suffered violence, and it is the violent who take it by force."

8. Final Hurdle?

Wrest from me, by firm and simple trust and persistent prayer, the treasures of My Kingdom. Such wonderful things are coming to you, Joy— Peace— Assurance— Security— Health— Happiness— Laughter.

Claim big, really big things now. Remember nothing is too big. Satisfy the longing of My Heart to give. Blessing, abundant blessing, on you both now and always. Peace.

After the second email that I responded to (each paragraph, with sarcastic, yes, cynical responses, having no idea where they were coming from)—I panicked and asked God to help me, please, to understand, since I knew this was "not right," especially when I actually mocked my ex-husband's accusations. The Lord then showed me a vision of the powerful Elijah, exhibited when he was high atop the city—**mocking** the Baal priests. When I went to look it up, I first stumbled onto the book of Second Kings, entitled, "Judgment upon Ahab's House."

Chapter 10, Verse 10 said something incredible, "Know then that there shall fall to the earth nothing of the word of the LORD, which the LORD spoke concerning the house of Ahab, for the LORD has done what He spoke through His servant Elijah." This was almost identical to what the Lord had spoken to me two years ago when my ex-husband had left. I should have known it was actually written in the Bible.

Yet, the verse that helped me the most was the last battle, the final hurdle that Elijah was to overcome, as described in First Kings under the heading, "God or Baal." "It came about at noon, that Elijah *mocked* them [the prophets of Baal] and said, 'Call out with a loud voice, for he is a god [Baal whom they served]; either he is occupied or gone aside, or is on a journey, or perhaps he is asleep and needs to be awakened'" (1 King 18:27). Was it Elijah, or was it God who spoke *through* Elijah?

"Why are the nations in an uproar and the peoples devising a vain thing? The kings of the earth take their stand and the rulers take counsel together against the LORD and against His anointed, saying, 'Let us tear their fetters apart and cast away their cords from us!' He who sits in the heavens laughs, the *Lord scoffs* at them. Then He will speak to them in His anger and terrify them in His fury" (Psalm 2:1–5).

The way I was responding was not in a manner that I felt comfortable with, because I'm so comfortable living "Peacefully." But was my *peace* at any cost?

While speaking to my children, the Lord showed me the headlines that I had read as a teenager, which covered the front page of every newspaper—"America Held Hostage"—which was about one of our US presidents, who was mocked at the time, saying he a coward, because he allowed this atrocity, by giving in to the threats imposed. As I read it, I heard God ask me if being a coward is what I would choose for my children or the women who I was hoping to encourage. Or, would I instead encourage others, by my own example, to move fearlessly toward the battle? What would I choose, if I had to make a choice?

It was then that the Lord showed me something I had never seen before. During my reply to my ex-husband (when I said that I would *no longer* comply with *any* more of his threats regarding what I could publish or post on the RMI website—which he was reading daily—so it would be futile for him to threaten me again), that's when I realized that **I had unknowingly continued to allow my ex-husband to run the ministry God gave me**—and even to control portions of RMI—that's how far reaching my complying to threats could go!

Something else I'd like to share…several years ago, I heard something that the author John Bevere said while speaking at our church, and it made a deep impression on me. He said, "If you do not use the God-given authority that He gave you, someone else will take it and use it *against* you!"

This is not to say that I had done the wrong thing, when I didn't fight my ex-husband, when he blocked my eCommerce website almost immediately after the divorce (or it may even have been *before* the divorce was final. I can't remember now.) Nor was it that God was telling me that I should have called the police and had my ex-husband arrested (as so many of my friends and family members had begged me to do), when he came to my warehouse while I was traveling and destroyed cases of RMI's books, devotionals and videotapes that I bought to sell. No, it was not a mistake, but now things were different—this, as I said, I believe and hope is my final hurdle that was looming in front of me.

There was another thing the Lord showed me that shocked me. It concerned my new friendship with my ex-husband and his wife (and their children), which is why I was caught so off-guard by this vile letter. Again, while asking for "a word, just a word," since I was so sure and terrified that I had fallen out of favor or intimacy with the Lord, I was not understanding why I responded the way that I did to his letters full of accusations and threats, rather than just ignore or agree.

It was then that I simply opened my Bible to see "Alliance Displeases God." While reading on, it stated in 2 Chronicles 20:35, "After this Jehoshaphat king of Judah *allied himself* with Ahaziah king of Israel. He acted *wickedly* in so doing." This was done by the same king who had earlier prayed, "Should evil come upon us, the sword, or judgment, or pestilence, or famine, we will stand before this house and before You (for Your name is in this house) and cry to *You* in our distress, and *You* will hear and deliver us" (2 Chronicles 20:9).

This verse then led me to remember one of my favorite passages of the Bible, when King Asa makes the same foolish mistake by seeking the friendship with his enemies, rather than trusting God to deliver. "For the eyes of the Lord move to and fro throughout the whole earth that He may **strongly support** those whose **heart** is completely His. You have acted foolishly in this. Indeed, *from now on you will surely have wars"* (2 Chronicles 16:9).

Yet, even seeing these verses that came to mind instantly each time I asked the Lord for confirmation that what I was doing *was* **His** plan, I still felt unsure, since the way I have been living for the past sixteen years of my life has been the exact opposite of what I was doing now. For more than a decade, my very nature has been transformed; my whole being has been made new. "Behold, I am making **all things new**" (Revelations 21:5). "And I will give them one **heart**, and put a **new** spirit within them. And I will take the **heart** of stone out of their flesh and give them a **heart** of flesh" (Ezekiel 11:19).

While writing this chapter, the Lord brought to mind and led me to read a verse that most of us know, but I have never actually quoted. It is, from the wisest man, Solomon, when he tries to explain that there is a *time* for everything. He says,

"There is an appointed time for everything.

And there is a time for every event under heaven—

A time to give birth and a time to die;

> A time to plant and a time to uproot what is planted.

A time to kill and a time to heal;

> A time to tear down and a time to build up.

A time to weep and a time to laugh;

> A time to mourn and a time to dance.

A time to throw stones and a time to gather stones;

> A time to embrace and a time to shun embracing.

A time to search and a time to give up as lost;

> A time to keep and a time to throw away.

A time to tear apart and a time to sew together;

> A time to be silent and a time to speak.

A time to love and a time to hate;

> A time for war and a time for peace" (Ecclesiastes 3:1-8).

8. Final Hurdle?

Just as I had shared time and again in all my books, a good way to see if what you are doing (or you are about to do) is of God, is to ask yourself if it feels good to your flesh, or, does it need the help of the Holy Spirit to carry it out? Without a doubt, my flesh cringed at the thought of saying anything remotely close to what I wrote in each of my email replies.

Though we are all born with a sinful, angry nature, once refined (a process that often takes years, as it did with me), that person is no longer the same. For too many of you, telling your ex-husband off would *feel* great! And, as I said, it is really not about what we do, since many of us don't say something, due to fear or because we worry about what other people would think of us.

What the Lord is showing all of us is simply this: what we do, or what someone else does, cannot be *judged* by what we see. That's why we must *never* judge anyone or anything that a person does, because what we don't see (the reason behind their actions) is really what counts. It is what God sees, and how He tests us, to see if we are real. Or maybe it is more so that He can show **us** what we are really all about. "The refining pot is for silver and the furnace for gold, but the LORD *tests* **hearts**" (Proverbs 17:3).

Initially, I didn't *want* to respond. Then, once written, I didn't *want* to send it, mainly due to fear and concern about what others would think of me. Surely, I believed myself to have left these shortcomings long ago, but they are still present in my life, and both are character flaws that will hold me back from the place and position where God has called me. The same goes for anything God continues to bring to the surface in your life.

These are, hopefully, the final hurdles that you need to get over, in order to move your mountain. But once you get over this, you will find you are left with emotions, those feelings, which must be channeled toward the right frequency of energy that will ultimately make or break your mountain.

But before going to the next chapter, let me share just one more thing. For you to come to the place where you can move a mountain, you have to come right up to it. When you are miles from the final hurdle, the height and magnitude of your mountain may look large, but not the way it does when you are standing at the foot of it. Standing there, at the very bottom, you look up to see your mountain is HUGE. Standing there, you see there is no other way around it; it has to move.

God purposely brings us smack up in front of it: there's no money left in your account; there's no possible cure; there's no way to contact your loved-one—the impossibilities are endless, and you are out of ideas to know how to deal with it.

For the wicked man to be no more, the wickedness needed (and still needs) to increase. There is no other way. "Yet a little while and the **wicked man** will be **no more**; and you will look carefully for his place and he will **not** be there" (Psalm 37:10). "How great are Your works, O LORD! Your thoughts are very deep. A senseless man has no knowledge, nor does a stupid man understand this: That when the wicked sprouted up like grass and all who did iniquity flourished, *it was only that they might be destroyed forevermore*" (Psalm 92:5–7).

This is the way God works—He purposely allows everything to become impossible. He also waits until the last moment to move: didn't He wait until the last moment with the honeymoon that was going to be lost, only to "at the last minute" turn it into the blessing of a romantic wedding and honeymoon for my son and his fiancé?

All of you have your own "last minute" and "things got worse" testimonies, so rehearse them now. And if you tend to struggle regularly, be sure to write them down, and, better yet, submit your praise like I do to RMIEW's website, so the whole world will know how "nothing is impossible with God"—not even the final, unexpected, hurdle.

Chapter 9

Feelings

"The **feelings** I get when I see the high **mountain** ranges —
stirrings of desire, longings for the heights—
Remind me of You, and I'm spoiled for anyone else!"
—Song of Solomon 7 MSG

Feelings, wow, these emotions can make or break us; have you noticed? Women were once very careful to keep their feelings hidden, kept very much to themselves. Just watch older movies to get a sense of how different women used to be. But now, the woman of this century is not only allowing her feelings to be known, but her emotions are given full reign over everything. Feelings and emotions are allowed to take over and rule, or should I say *ruin,* her life. The primary reasons our emotions are destructive, I believe, is because we have no idea how much power our emotions possess, once again, for good or for evil. So, we use them unwisely, or should I say, they use and soon destroy us and everything we hold dear to us.

Women, in particular, are made up of many feelings that are generated by our emotions, and these emotions create the highs and lows in our lives. But what if we could actually learn to *benefit* from our emotions, by using our feelings as a barometer? This is the purpose of this chapter: to help each of us learn how to measure the changes in our emotional pressure, which will indicate that our spiritual atmosphere is changing and will show up in our feelings; we must redirect them toward the good, rather than the bad.

Recently women have taken a beating, in regard to their emotions. It really wasn't that long ago, when a woman simply hid or controlled her feelings totally and completely in public, and even privately; however, it may very well have been that extreme that ushered in the complete opposite, which is now to "let it **all** out." Many women, today, are literally out of control when it comes to their feelings—if so, she is being totally manipulated by her emotions, rather than using them, as I believe, God intended.

Well then, should we simply *control* our feelings, or should we, instead, learn to *use* how we feel, so that we can actually benefit from our emotions?

In the beginning of the Feminist Movement, many women (who were trying to prove that a woman was every bit like a man) began to deny that they had any emotions or feelings at all. These women stuffed their emotions and feelings down, only for them to erupt a few decades later into the foolish antics we see on television and in movies today. No one would have imagined how reality shows would not just foster bad behavior but encourage it. How many of us have seen at least one of the very popular reality shows that depict the sorry state of women who are completely out of control—their emotions flying everywhere for the world to see, and they are not one bit ashamed? Read what the Bible says, "'Were they ashamed because of the abomination they have done? They were not even ashamed at all; they did not even know how to **blush**. Therefore they shall fall among those who fall; at the time that I punish them, they shall be cast down,' says the LORD" (Jeremiah 6:15).

Knowing that women were created, uniquely, *with* emotions, it is therefore extremely important for us to understand these emotions and then use them—by redirecting them in the proper way. In addition, once you share your feelings with someone, the emotions have escaped; it will mean dealing with them again and again and again. I've taught my children, especially my daughters (due to how we women are notorious for sharing our emotions too openly), **never to speak about anything when there are negative emotions attached to them.** Instead, like a storm, negative emotions will soon pass, and once they are again stable, only then is it safe to share them.

So, when do our emotions begin to run havoc in our lives? For many women, it is when someone has hurt us, often through rejection. However, for most women, it is due to being *denied* what we want, when we believe we **deserve better.** This is especially true, when we, as Christians, believe that someone or something is standing in the way of our miracle! We all *feel* that, don't we?

So then, what are we, as godly Christian women, women who "smile at the future," women who exhibit a "gentle and quiet spirit," supposed to do with our very *real* feelings? One way is to use a principle that I wrote about in a previous chapter, when my son's fiancé believed the miracle of getting married was from God, but her desires didn't match up with the authority over her. When someone is in our way (or maybe it's just *our* limited ability to make something happen), when it's what we truly believe God wants us to do or have, then that's when God is just asking us to *ponder* these desires in our hearts. The many times I've done this, I sense it's almost tenderizing my heart.

*Difficult to do? Yes, but oh so powerful! That's because, once these desires are hidden from plain view and not spoken of freely, they are then put in a place where God visits. And He is there, in order to *give* us our most secret and precious desires! Remember? "Delight yourself in the Lord; And He will *give you* the *desires* of your heart" (Psalm 37:4). Going beyond this, while looking up this verse, I read the entire Psalm that truly blessed me. Read it yourself, because it confirms so much of what has already been said. Read it slowly:

"Do not fret [to be worried, irritated, or agitated about something] because of evildoers, be not envious toward wrongdoers. For they will wither quickly like the grass and fade like the green herb. Trust in the LORD and do good; dwell in the land and cultivate faithfulness. **Delight yourself in the LORD; and He will give you the desires of your heart.** Commit your way to the LORD, trust also in Him, and *He will do it.* He will bring forth your righteousness as the light and your judgment as the noonday.

"**Rest** in the LORD and wait patiently for Him; do not fret because of him who prospers in his way, because of the man who carries out wicked schemes. Cease from anger and forsake wrath; do not fret; it leads only to evildoing. For evildoers will be cut off, but those who wait for the LORD, they will inherit the land. Yet a little while and the wicked man will be no more; and you will look carefully for his place and he will not be there. But the humble will *inherit the land* and will *delight* themselves in *abundant prosperity"* (Psalm 37:1–11).

Notice how the second paragraph begins with the word, rest. As a parent, I know that my children can't be expected to act their best when they are overly tired. We women also need rest, rest from our overworked emotions, and that rest can only be accomplished when we give each care (or worry or burden) to Him and when we simply "wait patiently for Him;" "and *He will do it.*"

Feelings to Move

Now, it's time to discuss how our feelings relate to moving mountains. Just like everything else, *resisting* (even *resisting* feelings, like fear) is not the right way to deal with these negative emotions—emotions that have the potential to do so much harm and stand in the way of our miracle. So, what can we do with this powerful, and often deadly (to a miracle) force, when our emotions try to overcome us? What I found, just recently, when a bout of fear kept flowing over me—fear that was trying to penetrate my heart—I chose, instead, to **use** those feelings, by modifying and actually redirecting fear into thrill and excitement. That's when I realized that I could actually *benefit from* them!

Have you ever noticed that fear and excitement are opposing emotions, and yet, they are really just a fine line apart? There are some people who love to ride a rollercoaster, for example, because of the thrill of it. Then there are others, like me, who don't feel a thrill, but, instead, feel nothing but fear. Our emotions, simply a fine line apart, are very similar. What is different is in our *perception* of what we are experiencing. And a lot of how we *perceive* something is due to how *much* we think about it, but more important is in what way we think about it.

For instance, I doubt that many of the young people in line at the amusement park are thinking of how well the coaster is built, but I would be; therefore, my perception would result in fear.

The verses we just read above (Psalm 37) point to the very same thing, which is: how we *think* about things. For instance, do we think about how much money we don't have to pay for something or what people are going to think about us when they find out about something we did or didn't do? The list is endless to what we might fret about, which may even lead us to doing something evil or wrong. And even if we don't resort to actually doing something wrong, fear alone, as most of us have learned, is actually the opposite of faith, which means we are not pleasing God when we fear. The Bible says, "without faith it is impossible to please God" (Hebrews 11:6).

Just recently, I faced quite a few mountains that loomed over my life, and each time I found that the fear of what *might* happen next, or what *might* be the result of my actions, stood in the way of moving that mountain, due entirely to how I felt. **What I found was that if I took a step back, and then refocused on the *thrill* of what I knew (in faith) was about to happen, I could use those feelings to fuel the spiritual strength needed to move the mountain through the positive force of faith.**

It is when we choose to turn our eyes from what *appears* to be happening, and instead look at what He has already done for us (and others) in the past, that our perception changes. Thinking over in our minds all the other mountains that He moved begins to thrill and excite us. And that's when we are able to turn our doubt into real strength—mountain moving strength.

Now, let's take the principle a bit higher, by also reminding ourselves, and Him, of the promises that He has made to us—even promises He may have made to you and me *years ago*. These promises (added to what He's done) will further increase our faith and move those feelings from fear to excitement, and we will have the thrill of watching another mountain be thrown into the sea!

As I said, the Lord saw fit to bring one mountain after another into my life just recently. And each time I told myself that if I truly believed, then I would not be frightened or worried, but I would be excited—therefore, I needed to let my feelings reflect what I believed.

That's when my feelings became my barometer and a way to let me know just how I was thinking about those mountains and whether or not my mountain was going to move or continue to loom.

Another import aspect is knowing that the *absence of fear* can move your mountain. Almost all of the testimonies of restored marriages are from women who came to the place where they no longer *feared* being alone, nor *feared* their husbands might not come back to them. Once they experienced having a heavenly Husband and His love, once they knew they'd never be alone, that's when there was no more fear. Once *fear* was gone, almost *instantly* they saw their situations turn around, and their husbands' hearts were turned back to them.

It happened exactly like that both times with me. The first time my husband left, my entire life was consumed with fear. It took almost two years to rid myself of unimaginable fear (of being a single mother alone with small children and often thinking of how it would adversely affect them growing up). It wasn't until I came to the place where there was no fear at all (all due to knowing and experiencing an amazing intimacy with the Lord), then, once my all-consuming fear was gone, my husband returned almost immediately.

The second time he left and filed for divorce, I didn't fear at all (this time due to an even greater intimacy with the Lord, which was at an all-time high)—even though I had much more to lose the second time. Instead of fear, I rested in my trust, knowing more fully of His goodness and always looking for the good in what was happening. These dictated my emotions. The result of absolutely no fear, which was replaced by excitement, turned my husband's heart around almost instantaneously, in equal measure.

The question I have is, was the immediate change due to how I felt? Or is it something the other person can sense, like we all read in Erin's marriage restoration books? Can it be that our negative emotions, like fear, are an unseen energy force that God created and (countless times) has warned us **not** to allow into our lives, because it is what will inhibit our God-given moving mountain power?

9. Feelings

The song made popular in the eighties says, "Feelings, *nothing more than feelings...?*" Though we try to dismiss the importance of how we feel, our feelings just might be the deciding factor to whether or not our mountain moves, or whether it appears to grow larger and wider than it was before. What we believe in our hearts will determine how we think and will result in how we *feel* about that mountain.

For instance, if we believe during surgery that our doctor knows what he is doing and the surgery will go well, it will alleviate our fears, which we now know results in a better outcome and quicker healing. What multiplies the outcome is when Christians put their trust in God, who is in complete and utter control. However, if we instead begin thinking of and rehearsing all the possible complications, the many risks, and what *could* potentially go wrong, our feelings will be much different—we will be overcome with fear! Fear, the Bible tells us at least three times, is how we open the door to whatever it is that we are fearful of, to be allowed to enter our lives.

"For what I **fear** *comes upon* me, and what I dread befalls me" (Job 3:25).

"**Fear** and trembling *come upon* me, and horror has overwhelmed me" (Psalm 55:5).

"What the wicked **fears** will *come upon* him, but the desire of the righteous will be granted" (Proverbs 10:24).

So, we see that *what* we meditate on (fearful thoughts or faithful thoughts) has the ability to be manifested in our lives, and *our feelings* are the barometer to know what we are actually allowing into our lives and what ultimately lies up ahead for us.

Lack and Fear

Fear is what turned the tide of prosperity to lack, in my life. And when I say prosperity, I am not only speaking in regard to finances, but in every area of my life.

The lack that came into my life, I can now clearly see, began with a series of events while I was traveling. An event broke into my haven of rest, faith, and tranquility—the peace that surpasses all understanding that I had been enjoying. It began while I was in Africa, on the very tip of the continent, in Cape Town. For the first time since I left home weeks earlier, I was finally able to speak to my daughter, who had gone to live with her dad just before I left. Though I was extremely happy to hear her voice, it made the reality of "losing her" very real.

Once we hung up, I headed to my room, anticipating a great night's sleep, since I was going to be flying back to Johannesburg the next morning. I needed sleep; I was scheduled to speak there when I arrived. However, in the next room, there was a wild party going on, with people or furniture constantly hitting the wall, loud voices and yelling, and worse, cigarette smoke that began filling *my* room. There was not another available room in the hotel, and even though I called the management, the party continued throughout the night.

Solomon, who is said to be the wisest man who ever lived, told us to be careful to "Catch the **foxes** for us, the **little foxes** that are ruining the vineyards, while our vineyards are in blossom" (Song of Solomon 2:15). Though I had been through so much, and in comparison this was nothing at all but a bit of lost sleep, it proved to be that little fox that I was unable to catch. It wasn't this alone; it was also immediately after the reality of my daughter not living with me hit me, and I'd not taken time to speak to my HH or her Father about it. Once the door of fear was wide open, one fear leading the way to another. Fear led to me worrying about my very short flight. More fear led to me missing my scheduled flight, which put me on another flight that took off in a horrendous thunder storm.

And by the way, did you know that **defeat** is what often *follows* great victories and hits very powerful men and women? Here are a couple of examples. First is Jonah, who saved the entire nation of Nineveh from destruction. Then, right after this huge victory, he says, "Therefore now, O LORD, please *take my life* from me, for death is better to me than life" (Jonah 4:3). Most of his despair was due to Jonah's feelings for the ungodly people, who God chose to spare.

Another example is Elijah, one of the most powerful prophets, who also was consumed right after his amazing victory—when 450 Baal prophets had been destroyed. Afterward, "he himself went a day's journey into the wilderness, and came and sat down under a juniper tree; and he requested for himself that he might die, and said, 'It is enough; now, O LORD, *take my life,* for I am not better than my fathers'" (1 Kings 19:4).

Though I never quite got to the point of wanting the Lord to take my life, unlike these two men. I, nevertheless, can see how anyone is capable of plummeting into despair, after experiencing a great spiritual victory, all due to negative feelings that were not redirected back toward faith.

It was not even a week ago that my feelings, due primarily to what you read in the previous chapter, began to escalate in a negative way. I began worrying that I had "blown it," and therefore, I was not going to see my mountain move, and the feelings of fear started to wage war against my faith. Thankfully, due much to writing this chapter, my feelings proved to be the barometer that told me that if I was going to see the mountain fall in my life, I was going to have to **redirect my worrying into positive excitement, with anticipation and expectancy.** Yet, the way I was feeling was so low that I hadn't the emotional strength to turn the tide of my emotions. So, as a bride, I simply discussed everything with my HH and asked Him to do just that—I asked Him to turn my feelings of fear to excitement, and He did!

Prior to my feelings changing, the Lord had opened my eyes to the fact that I was at the end of this leg of my journey and that I mustn't give up. He told me that many saints gave up, just before they reached their goal, the destination, and that my erratic feelings were proof that things were near the end of my mountain moving. Even though my head knew this was true, my feelings prevented me from turning the negative force into positive feelings, and it's why I immediately spoke to my HH, before they could become rooted and take hold of me.

Almost immediately, I got up to shower and face the day with expectancy and anticipation! Did my day run smoothly? Absolutely not; instead, it was a day full of hundreds of tests, trials and temptations, but I continued to use each trial to fuel my faith, knowing that it proved I was just a short distance away from my mountain of debt falling into the sea. Then came the test.

There were actually three large amounts of money that I needed to sow as my test. My fear and feelings of "lack" wanted me to pull back, but the eyes of faith and trust told me to move forward. The enemy had made sure that, just the day before, I *saw* that I had nothing left in my accounts and my credit cards were all maxed out. Nevertheless, I had to move forward. While dressing, the Lord asked me how I *really* believed: Did I truly believe that my accounts, which I *saw* were empty, were actually attached into Him and His unending source? Or, did I believe what I saw? Did I really believe that He would lead me along this path and not provide the testimony of no debt? I knew that the result of how I felt, and what I did that day, is what would determine whether my mountain of debt would fall.

Each test, trial and temptation served to strengthen my faith in all He has done for me and will continue to do for me. Though my overflow of blessings has not yet manifested, I can *feel* that "it is finished" and that it is only a matter of time when I see, and I can announce, that my mountain of debt has fallen. I don't know how it will happen, any more than I know when, but nevertheless, it **is** about to happen—I can feel it.

Dear bride, our feelings may just be the most powerful force that can cause you and me to soar like eagles, or cause us to want to bury ourselves below the face of the earth.

Knowing their power, we, therefore, need to pay close attention to our spiritual barometer, which shows up in our feelings, and when we feel the barometer falling, speak to our HH and shelter ourselves under the Almighty—not waiting until they take root and grab hold of us. Keeping negative feelings hidden, we must then cover our negative feelings with His promises and ponder deeply what He has done for us (and others) in the past.

With our minds renewed, we then must *simply speak* what is hidden deep in our hearts, which is reflected in our *feelings,* so that our mountain will move in the right direction—toward the sea, and no longer casting shadows on our world.

Chapter 10
Mountains to Climb

"Listen! My beloved! Behold, He is coming,
Climbing on the mountains,
Leaping on the hills!"
—Song of Solomon 2:8

When faced with difficulties in my life, my spiritual theme song always used to be "Climb *Every* Mountain," which many of us heard in the movie *The Sound of Music*. Then one day, I learned that God often meant for us to **move** those mountains, rather than to be so quick to climb them. Though this book is about moving mountains, I have found, however, that there *are* some mountains that block our way that God may have *meant* for us to climb. What exactly do I mean?

You've heard of people who one day go to the altar and are not only gloriously saved, they are instantly delivered from some sin or disease. Yet, in the same church, there are other poor souls who have believed God for years to be delivered from something but are instead called to work through it—in other words, climb their mountain. How many of you, who are Restoration Fellowship members, have had an ePartner who reads just part of the restoration materials, and she instantly gets her marriage restored (within weeks or months of applying them half-heartedly) while you, on the other hand, have been working through the principles, and dying to self, for years?

In this chapter I realized again that God does not always ask us to move every mountain, but will, in fact, sometimes call us to climb it. In chapters 5 and 6 of this book, you learned about the honeymoon that did not take place but was miraculously transferred to another son, but what you didn't know about was what triggered a chain of events, which became a mountain He asked me to climb.

After witnessing such a magnificent mountain falling into the sea just days earlier, which created an atmosphere of faith so thick you could feel it, I was overflowing with faith that was at an all-time high. However, with one mountain safely in the sea, its absence revealed a new and larger mountain. What was worse is that, as I spoke to this new mountain, it did not fall but stood higher and more foreboding than anything I thought I would ever have to tackle in my lifetime. It knocked me harder than anything, and I mean anything, that I have lived through thus far in my life.

Having been in ministry for so many years (almost two decades now), and the majority of it spent in sowing into helping marriages for most of those years, I always told the Lord the same thing, "If I have gained any rewards at all, then let these rewards be applied to my children—by blessing them with good marriages." In addition, I (through the grace of God) did all the "right things" when raising them. I know that many of you were not Christians when you raised your children, and often you find that you are reaping some tremendous difficulties that you can merit to what you had sown. However, what if you *apparently* did everything right, but then you still find that things are not happening according to *your* plan, or should I say *your* plans for *your* children?

Prior to my sons marrying, I had real doubts, mostly due to the "sins of the father" on our side, and on the other side (of one) there was a pattern of a mother leaving husbands and repeatedly remarrying. One day, I sat down with this couple to share my concerns that they would fall into the same sins—unless they completely trusted and relied on God. I remember my son saying, "Mom, you're scaring me," and I replied, "Then use it to remain motivated to trust God—because your marriage will end in divorce if He doesn't stop it."

Though I had God's *promises* that He would **bless** my children, I had dozens of promises I believed for them, along with what I thought was a good amount of sowing strong principles into each of their lives. Plus, I had the promise of training my children the way they should go: Proverbs 22:6. To me, there was no doubt in my mind that I had my children's futures all sown up, and yet, I saw this mountain that was clearly there in my son and his soon-to-be bride's life.

When some issues began to appear, coupled with our concerns, I knew all I had to do was watch and wait for God to stop the marriage that was so risky. Not only did I have superb faith, but so did his siblings. Unfortunately, I heard that one went to talk to his brother and tell him that, in light of what was already happening, he simply couldn't marry her. Yet, my son said he was committed.

Years ago, I learned, and then taught women, that when you try to stand in the way of wickedness, it only increases the intensity for them to seek what you are trying to block. However, with what I learned and understood, with the lack of faith that I once possessed, I would have panicked, thinking that my son (by speaking to his brother) had caused it to happen for sure, rather than stopping it. Yet, instead of worrying, I knew that when it is God's will, and we simply want His will above anything else, then our trust in Him will cause right to overrule the wrong. Did you know that?

Goodness, mercy, righteousness, all the things that come from God are so much more powerful than evil. There is simply no contest, none. As a matter of fact, God's power of goodness is so great that He can take the bad and turn it around for good, based on just one promise: Romans 8:28, "And we know that God causes all things to work together for good to those who love God, to those who are called according to His purpose." Now I find that this verse is the story of my life. God has allowed the sins of relationships to invade my life *on purpose,* to show me, and you, the power of His taking things that are bad and turning them for good.

Whether or not God chose to turn anything for good, I knew what I had to do: once married, both of my sons' brides would be my daughters, just as if I had given birth to each one of them. Both of them would each be "one with their husbands," my sons.

10. Mountains to Climb

And so, according to His perfect plan, both weddings took place as planned, just a day apart.

It was only after they were married that God reminded me about King David, who had appealed to God for mercy to save his dying son. Everyone panicked when they heard that his son had, indeed, died and wondered what kind of "madman" David would become, because they had seen how he reacted to his illness. But instead, they found David dressed and in good spirits. David explained that when there was a chance that God would hear him, he would lament, but when he saw that God had made His decision, by his son dying, then it was no longer time to mourn.

This was the way God was telling me how we all were to conduct ourselves (my children and myself), once the marriage had taken place. God had made His decision, knowing there was more than enough faith, more than enough time, more than enough opportunity to stop the marriage, if it had been His will. But He hadn't, so we knew for certain that this was HIS plan for my son to marry. Our only response had to be to embrace, with compassionate love, God's choice for my son's wife. Though I had my doubts, concerns and fears, over time, I discovered that this young woman was His clear choice and who would complete my son. It just took time for this truth to unfold, after watching my son be asked to climb a similar mountain to mine.

Yet, at the time, within an hour of the realization that my son had actually married, which meant that the mountain had not fallen into the sea, I sat in my room, alone, stunned as the reality of it all became just too real, and my tears began to give way.

It took only a few minutes for my tears to stop, when I heard the Lord's still, small, sweet voice say, "Are you done? Now, tell me *why* you are crying?" If you heard this, you may dismiss it as a sign that this is not God talking to you at all, since, of course, He **knows** "why" (He knows everything); so why would He ask? But that is just biblical ignorance. You don't have to get far in the Bible to read that God called to Adam and Eve, when they had sinned and were hiding, asking them, "Where are you?" when, of course, He knew right where they were.

Knowing His question was more for me than it was for Him, I had to ask myself why. Why *was* I crying? So, I answered Him saying, "Because I didn't want it to turn out **this** way." "What way *did* you want it to turn out, Michele?" I really couldn't express it, so He went on and asked me, "Was it that your son would live 'happily ever after'—is that how?" Yes, that was really it. I wanted all of my children to have happy marriages: free from all the junk I had fought so hard to not give to them. Yes, that was it.

Yet the Lord pressed further, deep into the depths of my heart, when He asked, "Is this *really* what you've always wanted?" His question made me dig a bit deeper into the recesses of my heart (that was terribly hurt), when I said, "What I really want, and what has been my passion for as long as I can remember, is that my children have a walk and intimacy with You, my Darling, like no one who has walked the face of this earth. I want them to go beyond where I have gone. That is what I want above anything else."

My Husband then asked, "And how do you experience this kind of intimacy? Is it by living 'happily ever after'? Or will deep intimacy with Me develop by traveling *through* the difficult valleys and experiencing pain that you have experienced?" I didn't have to answer. I knew how my son would experience the closeness I wanted for him. I knew the only way to learn was to hold onto and embrace His Father—which would happen during the very tough times—valleys, I sensed, He wanted me to know were up ahead.

Yes, my son knows Him well, but not in the way that those of us who have held the hand of sorrow and suffering know Him. And, yes, this *is* what I wanted for him. Yes, this *is* the mountain that my son was chosen to climb, and I, too, will climb a parallel mountain as I watch him, silently.

Conclusion

In all my seeking, the Lord has opened my eyes to some incredible things that all of us need to look at, when we have a mountain that fails to move but, instead, is a mountain we are called to climb.

First, how many of you have had an "unplanned" or even "unwanted" pregnancy, only to find that, once your unwanted or unplanned child was born, that child was more of a blessing than you could have ever imagined? Not only did it change you, and improve your quality of life, but it also changed your entire family and everyone whose life that child of yours touched.

This also happens with children who are taken from us prematurely: it changes our family, often an entire community, and sometimes the world, but especially—us. Though we would *never* have chosen that path or circumstance for ourselves, it was something that, though difficult, changes lives and makes us forever different.

How many of you have a child that was injured or harmed physically, mentally and/or emotionally, either in the womb, during childbirth, as a baby, in their early years, or maybe just recently? I can say with a small measure of experience that these children are so trying, and take so much additional energy, that it keeps us clinging onto God— but that's the point, isn't it? So much of the heartache is due to our wanting that child to be made right or made whole; however, in most of the cases that I know or have personally experienced—I see in these special children a "childlikeness" that causes them to be especially sensitive to the things of God, spiritual things, and an intimacy that very few of us realize in our lifetime.

Since this is what we, as Christian mothers, desire more than anything in the world for our children (to know and experience the Lord in a supernatural way), then in many ways, these children are the ones we should be the happiest for, shouldn't we? And yet, we can't help wishing, hoping, praying, and yearning that God would heal them, make them whole, so that their "quality" of life might be like everyone else's, like our other children perhaps. Here I am speaking to you, when the truth is, I am speaking to myself as a mother.

It might be that healing or being made whole has nothing at all to do with my children or yours, but it has everything to do with you and me. Whether it is in dealing with someone in your family or if it actually is you who needs to be healed and made whole, God has a road to health and healing that I personally have been asked to travel along for quite some time. But that is another book perhaps. Coming back to this topic...

Though the wife my son married caused me great concern, and their marriage was a mountain I desperately wanted to send to the depths of the sea, I know full well that she will end up being the most blessed "unplanned" event, who will turn out to be the daughter of my dreams. Her presence in my son's life, in my family's life, and especially in my life, I'm certain, will prove to be what changes us and increases our quality of life—I know, because it already has! One of its first blessings has been in watching my children accept and love (beyond measure) their new sisters, both in exactly the same way, which I can't even express on paper.

This mountain is one that my son is just beginning to climb and one that I am now excited to climb by his side, silently watching. I know how it will change all of us, by creating the greatest of intimacy with my HH and their Father, which truly has been, and will always be, the deepest desire of my heart.

Epilog to this Chapter

Soon after my son and his wife were married, they were blessed with a son. Months later, just as I'd forewarned, my daughter-in-law left my son and filed for divorce. Remember what I said prior to the conclusion? When I said, "I, too, will climb a parallel mountain, as I watch him, silently." I suppose that was my mountain to climb. To watch but to remain silent, watching the suffering as my son lost his wife and baby boy. Nevertheless, even though my son never sat down and read the men's Restore Your Marriage book, I began to see how its truths were followed. I realized that as I lived and spoke about the principles so often, as my son was growing up, without planning to, he instinctively began following its principles.

Months after their divorce, after I was back living in the U.S. again, was when my son chose to confide in me. He shared how he'd "lost his faith" not in God, but in His desire to restore his marriage, after he'd fasted and begged God not to allow the divorce to go through. But it had. It was while I was in Europe that I experienced something quite similar, falling into applying a well-known belief that we needed to tell God what we wanted, claim it and it would happen. Yet, like my son, it hadn't happened and it completely broke me.

Sharing my understanding, because I really did understand, led to my son then opening up to me that he was at a loss to know what to do next. Because he asked, I knew it was time to help guide him the rest of the way. "…always being ready to make a defense to everyone who **asks** you to give an account for the **hope** that is in you, yet with gentleness and reverence" (1 Peter 3:13-15).

I explained that He would create a type of crisis, allowing him to follow the Lord and navigate through it using wisdom, and it would result in God restoring his marriage. A crisis did follow just days later, and even though I was speaking, sharing principles and listening to what my HH and His Father was saying, I did much more "watching" my son climb, until, I watched, we all watched, GOD restore his marriage. And, just as He promised, a double recompense followed. Not only was my son reunited with his son, soon after their restoration, God blessed them with a second son.

Today we all are one family, living under one large roof, closer than ever, with more love for each other—more than anything I could ever have dreamed way back while looking at a mountain that He meant for us to climb.

Ephesians 3:20, "Now to Him who is able to do far more abundantly beyond all that we ask or think, according to the power that works within us…"

TLB, "Now glory be to God, who by his mighty power at work within us is able to do far more than we would ever dare to ask or even dream of—infinitely beyond our highest prayers, desires,

The Message, "God can do anything, you know—far more than you could ever imagine or guess or request in your wildest dreams!"

And finally, Isaiah 30:18, "Therefore the LORD longs to be gracious to you, and therefore He *waits* on high to have compassion on you. For the LORD is a God of justice; how blessed are all those who long for Him."

Chapter 11

Tarry

"For the vision is yet for an **appointed time**,
But at the end it shall speak, and not lie:
Though it **tarry—wait** for it;
Because it will surely come, it will not **tarry**."
—Habakkuk 2:3 KJV

Did you know that your promise, or miracle, or mountain moving doesn't immediately reveal itself—even if it's been completed in the spiritual realm? Very often, there is a considerable waiting period for it to manifest itself in the natural in order, for us and everyone to see it.

There are references to this truth all throughout the Bible, and yet, when sitting in the midst of our wait, we very often forget that God is a God who usually instructs us to wait, and for very good reasons. The main reason is timing: "For the vision is yet for an **appointed time**, but at the end it shall speak, and not lie: though it **tarry**—**wait** for it; because it will surely come, it will not tarry" (Habakkuk 2:3 KJV). However, did you know that many Christians choose **not** to wait? We know this is true, because Paul wrote to the early church concerning this very thing. He said:

"Let us not lose heart in **doing** good, for in due time we will reap if we do not grow **weary**" (Galatians 6:9).

"But as for you, brethren, do not grow **weary** of **doing** good" (2 Thessalonians 3:13).

We see this truth even earlier in the Old Testament. Look what it says in this story about Daniel. "He said to me, 'O Daniel, man of high esteem, understand the words that I am about to tell you and stand upright, for I have now been sent to you.' And when he had spoken this word to me, I stood up trembling.

"Then he said to me, 'Do not be afraid, Daniel, for **from the *first* day** that you set your heart on understanding this and on humbling yourself before your God, your words were heard, and I have come in response to your words.

"But the prince of the kingdom of Persia was *withstanding* me for twenty-one days; then behold, Michael, one of the chief princes, came to help me, for I had been left there with the kings of Persia…**for the vision pertains to the days yet *future*"** (Daniel 10:11–14).

Rarely is the vision we see, or the promise that we receive, for right now. Though the urgency in our spirit, and the enthusiasm we feel, makes it appear as if the promise is for now, usually (maybe almost always) what we can easily envision and what He's promised us is for later, even much later, set for an "appointed" time.

If you're like me, it's while you and I are in the midst of that wait, while our mountain tarries, when we begin to wonder if we heard from the Lord correctly. We wonder if we have done everything right, and we wonder if this promise we have believed God for was really for us.

Yet, as the verse above bids us, we must not give up **"though it tarry—wait for it;** because *it will surely come,* it will not tarry [dawdle, delay or linger]" (Habakkuk 2:3). These were the instructions that Jesus gave to His disciples, when He knew they would need the Holy Spirit, its power, and its strength. The disciples had been told "it" "something" was going to come, but I am sure they had no idea what that "it" would really be.

After His death, during the time when He had reappeared to them in bodily form, "Gathering them together, He commanded them not to leave Jerusalem, but to **wait for** *what the Father had promised,* 'Which,' He said, 'you heard of from Me; for John baptized with water, but you will be baptized with the Holy Spirit *not many days* *from now'"* (Acts 1:4–5). Once again, it's important that you wait, no matter how long you wait.

What Are You Waiting For?

Over this past weekend, I was enormously blessed to attend a wedding that a very special and particular bride had waited for—for YEARS. The main reason she waited so long was due to the fact that she is an heiress, worth millions. Though she had been formally engaged at least twice before, each time, at the last minute each had been men marrying for money. So, with an intensely broken heart, along with her broken dreams, both weddings had been stopped by her father. When our family first met this dear young lady, she was just recovering from her second attempt at getting married, wanting desperately to be married like her younger sister.

As we became close friends, she confided in me that for years she wanted to believe that there was really someone out there for her, someone she could live with "happily ever after," but the right man eluded her. To help her wait, God had brought dozens of faithful people into her life to speak the truth, and I was blessed to be just one of them. For years, she and another close friend of mine studied *A Wise Woman*. [Our mutual friend was a strong believer in this workbook; having gone through the chapters with her ex-daughter-in-law, she was blessed to see her son's marriage restored and a restoration baby that soon followed, due to studying the truths in "Fruit of the Womb."]

They told me they met weekly, both determined that she would be the right wife when God sent her the right husband. Also, to help this happen, she came forward faithfully to pray at the altar, Sunday after Sunday, for that right man to come into her life. Then, just a few years ago, that "right man" seemed to appear, only to disappear just as quickly. Everyone was heartbroken for her once again.

Then, just this weekend, after all these years of waiting, after all the tears, every single sorrow vanished in an instant, and they were replaced with tears of joy, when we all sang the precious hymn

"Great is Thy Faithfulness" at her wedding. It seemed like a dream, when I watched the man whom God had chosen for her (a pastor of Teen Challenge, whose family had been praying for him for just as many years to find the "right woman"), her groom, look at her with the love in his eyes that I have rarely seen in a man, any man.

Update: The money this couple inherited had allowed them to devote themselves to philanthropic endeavors—by donating money to good causes that He laid on their hearts, often traveling together to some of the poorest areas of the world to put God's money to work.

Again, and again, we see that God truly is faithful; but unfortunately—no matter the strength of our own faith, no matter how many promises we compile—very often our miracles will continue to tarry long after we believed they would happen. Yet, once His promise shows up, I love how He is also faithful to be sure that those who invested in your mountain moving are there to rejoice with you. I am convinced that this is the entire reason for prayer and sowing into other people's lives—because it allows us to play a small role in God's miracle, giving us a front row seat. I believe that just as our tithe or offering is for us to join in and be part of life's changed investments (which always brings about dividends galore), so, too, are our prayers and our investments of time to teach others. When we pray, when we study alongside someone, we find ourselves rejoicing, just as if that miracle or mountain moving was happening to us!

Though I did not cry when my own sons married, I cried when this precious girl finally walked down the aisle to the tune of Twila Paris' song, "How beautiful the radiant bride who waits for her Groom with His light in her eyes." There were dozens of women and men who also cried, due to so many who'd invested into her life over her many years of waiting.

Why the wait? "Yet those who **wait** for the **LORD** Will gain new strength; they will mount up with wings like eagles, they will run and not get tired, they will walk and not become weary" (Isaiah 40:31).

Waiting on Us

Though we wonder why **we** are asked to wait upon the Lord, very often it's **us**, you and me, who the Lord is *waiting upon*. We see it in this verse from Isaiah: "Therefore the **LORD** *longs* [aches, yearns, craves] to be gracious to you, and therefore *He* **waits** on high to have compassion on you. For the **LORD** is a God of *justice*; how blessed are all those who long for Him" (Isaiah 30:18).

It's interesting that this verse tells us that the Lord is a God of justice, because that has been key to my faith in believing that God truly has plans to bless me beyond anything I could ever hope, dream or imagine! "For from days of old they have not heard or perceived by ear, nor has the eye **seen** a God besides You, Who acts in behalf of the one who **wait**s for Him" (Isaiah 64:4).

About a month ago, my youngest son said something "wasn't fair," and I agreed that usually things are not "fair," since God is not a God who is fair—thankfully—He is a God who is just. I went onto tell him how thankful we all should be that He is a God of justice, rather than fairness; and did he, my son, know the difference? He said that *fair* was when everyone got the same, but he thought *justice* meant getting punished.

Actually, I told him, and want to tell you, that God being a God of justice means that *eventually* (in the end) everyone gets what they deserve, good and bad. And that means that no matter what, it is always worth doing the **right thing,** no matter what the cost is now. Not only that, but when it seems that other people (especially your enemies) are getting blessed, and you're not, you can count on receiving, in the end, double. You need to wait with the expectation that something tremendously special *will* happen, especially if you have the right attitude when something happens that's unjust, because the right attitude is a reflection of the right heart.

No matter how long you wait, eventually the heavens **will** *open up* over your life and shower you with blessings that cannot compare to the suffering or difficulty that you went through. And all those difficulties you encountered along your journey will be a distant and foggy memory, if your heart has been kept right.

Time and again, when doubt would try to cause me to question what I have not yet seen—but what I truly believe, in faith, will happen, and happen soon—the Lord would remind me of the list of injustices that have come against me personally, come against my children, and come against my ministry, especially financially. Therefore, I have the security in knowing that very soon I will receive **double** what was lost or stolen from me—each and every injustice doubled.

"But you will be called the priests of the LORD; You will be spoken of as ministers of our God. You will eat the *wealth of nations,* and in their *riches* you will boast. Instead of your shame you will have a **double** portion, and instead of humiliation they will shout for joy over their portion. Therefore they will possess a **double** portion in their land, everlasting joy will be theirs. For I, the LORD, love justice, I hate robbery in the burnt offering; and I will faithfully give them their recompense and make an everlasting covenant with them" (Isaiah 61:6–8).

If you think this is amazing, He has more. He says that He will doubly bless our mistakes, yours and mine. Look what it says, "Speak kindly to Jerusalem; and call out to her, that her warfare has ended, that her iniquity has been removed, that she has received of the LORD'S hand **double** for all her sins" (Isaiah 40:2). And precious reader, remember, each and every one of these promises are for you, too. Simply believe them and acknowledge them, which means to speak each to your HH, so that you've officially claimed them. Personally, I acknowledge them by thanking my HH for what He's going to bless me doubly for.

Oh, and for those of you who were thinking that what we all **deserve** is hell; I agree. Yet, it is because of His righteousness that we benefit as we do, as partakers, meaning we get to share in His blessings. "For by these He has granted to us *His precious and magnificent* ***promises****,* so that by them you may become *partakers* of the divine nature, having escaped the corruption that is in the world by lust" (2 Peter 1:4).

"More than that, I count all things to be loss in view of the surpassing value of *knowing* **Christ Jesus my Lord,** for whom I have suffered the loss of all things, and count them but rubbish so that I may **gain Christ,** and may be found *in Him,* not having a righteousness of my own derived from the Law, but that which is *through faith in Christ,* the righteousness which comes from God *on the basis of faith,* that I may know Him and the power of His resurrection and the fellowship of His sufferings, being conformed to His death" (Philippians 3:8–10). Amen!

So, precious bride, just remember, what you are waiting for is **worth the wait.** For the vision that God gave you is still yet to come. It is scheduled for an *appointed time that* only God knows. But in the end, when it appears, it will speak and not lie of His faithfulness.

If you wait, when it appears, it will also prove that you were not crazy when you believed the impossible—that massive mountain moving. And though it tarries—be sure to wait for it—because *it will surely come;* it will not tarry forever!

Chapter 12

Teetering on the Brink of Prosperity

"But the humble will inherit the land
And will delight themselves in **abundant prosperity.**"
—Psalm 37:11

There's something about to take place in all of our lives—can you feel it? While at the same time, there's something also happening that is trying to stop it—can you see it?

Many have noticed both. Just recently I received an email from a friend saying that for the first time, she can't pay her taxes that are due. I've seen the same thing creeping up on many of the faithful women who tithe, but who are, for the first time, not able to pay their bills. Maybe you've gotten an overdraft notice from your bank; you've gotten a past due letter from your credit card or mortgage company. So, what's happening?

We are teetering on the brink of ruin or prosperity.

The question is, which way is our mountain going to fall: into the sea, or will it come crashing down on top of us? That's the picture the Lord gave me, when I asked Him to show me what's happening. We've envisioned our mountain of debt falling into the sea, seeing ourselves debt free and living in prosperity. Unfortunately, for some, the mountain is about fall forward on us. An avalanche of rock and mud, and with it all the dreams will be left under a pile of rubble, as we sit, surrounded by shame, pain, and confusion—wondering what happened.

12. Teetering on the Brink of Prosperity

Which way will your mountain fall?

Mine, I am determined, will fall into the sea. Though the enemy wants to use fear and intimidation to make me believe I am headed for ruin, not blessings, I refuse to believe it, and the way to prove my trust in Him is through my actions. The same goes for you; what you do is going to prove what you believe. It is not what we *say;* it's what we *do* that is the determining factor.

Yet, what we must do is terribly difficult, and for me to say it isn't difficult wouldn't be honest. When faced with financial and/or personal ruin, each of us must come, first, to the place of searching where **we** went wrong. It is called humility—a character quality that is almost absent in the world today. Unlike the Psalmist who asked God to "Search me, O God, and know my heart; try me and know my anxious thoughts; and see if there be any hurtful way in me, and lead me in the everlasting way" (Psalm 139:23–24), today most say "'I have done no wrong,'" as the adulteress said in Proverbs 30:20. Or they find someone or something else to blame.

Yet, this is not the characteristic of those who are His. Each time I have come up against something that has the potential to ruin me, I instinctively go to the Lord to see where *I have gone wrong*. Time and again, I'm thankful when He tells me that I have not made a mistake, but to simply trust Him. But when I began hearing that close friends of mine, whom I'd ministered to, were coming up financially short, unable to pay their bills, that's when the Lord CONVICTED me of where I had gone wrong.

There was no shame in the revelation, none at all; I felt only conviction. Conviction is different, because it's a strong desire to make things right at any cost, whereas "condemnation" is hopelessness coupled with blame and shame. Condemnation, therefore, is not from God. God convicts; the enemy condemns.

Immediately after I was convicted, suddenly, the light went on, and I realized that in my quest to move my mountain of debt, I failed to teach you, my readers (failing to feed the flock He has entrusted to me), the proper principles about giving. I failed to share with my closest friends the foundation to moving mountains of debt. Specifically, I failed to clearly explain that tithing begins with giving to your storehouse. I suppose that I assumed I was teaching you "by example" and that was enough. It wasn't. Not only did it prove to almost bankrupt my own ministry, even worse, it caused a lot of you (who were ignorant of this scheme of the enemy) to also come to the place of financial ruin or collapse, due primarily to a "lack of knowledge" when it comes to giving to your *storehouse*.

The only readers who are going to make it through, avoiding a catastrophe, are those who learned the principles and practiced the principles of giving to *your* storehouse, which comes with God's warranty—tithing and giving cheerfully equals prosperity! That's His promise.

Did you know that tithing is an act of obedience that always *appears* to be impossible to do? No one who faithfully tithes will tell you that it was easy when they began tithing. Every one of us looked at our income, what we brought in, and mentally (or often on paper) calculated, only to *see* immediately that **if** we tithed, we wouldn't be able to pay our bills. Yet, we each chose to trust God by what He SAID, not by what we SAW. That's called faith. "And without faith, it is impossible to please God..." (Hebrews 11:6 NIV).

So, once each of us stepped out and tithed to our storehouse, we discovered that, not surprisingly, we had **more** than enough! We found, time and again, we could not afford NOT to tithe!!

So, what then is your storehouse? Your storehouse is simply *where you are being spiritually fed*. Unfortunately, many of us begin tithing, then soon become legalistic and religious with *where* we tithe.

When I was going to church, I was being spiritually fed there, week after week, so it was easy to know *where* to tithe. Even though I wasn't fed well, I was fed. Yet, the real struggle came when I let go of my church, which is a struggle in and of itself. First you wonder what everyone, including yourself, will think, when you're not going

12. Teetering on the Brink of Prosperity 113

to church. That is followed by dealing with those who often begin to judge you.

Soon after I let go of my church, I got my first paycheck. So, like I do with everything, I simply asked my HH where to tithe. Immediately I heard, "Tithe to RMI." Yet I thought, "How stupid." First, it's not a church. Next, I thought, why would I take my paycheck from RMI (being my main income) only to turn around and give *back* a tenth? How ridiculous. But I went ahead and did it anyway, and that's when God confirmed to me that this was exactly what all pastors or people who work for churches do.

*Important note: One thing I learned early on from Erin is that following the Lord, and obeying God, often doesn't make sense. It's impossible to understand fully, until *after* you obey. Prior to being obedient (taking that step of faith), our minds are blind to understanding. Again, understanding fully only happens *after* you obey; that's when He will open your eyes to help you understand why, and it will make sense.

So, after I followed what He said, immediately I envisioned several of my previous pastors dropping their tithe in the offering, week after week, giving back to where they'd been paid. Thus, it wasn't a strange thing to do at all. Yet, I thought, it was easier for them. They tithe to a "real" church, with a real building. However, God showed me that RMI was my true *storehouse,* because RMI was where I was being fed.

When I was attending church, I only benefited slightly, twice a week. However, since coming to RMI, I was fed daily and fed with much more "meat," as it says in Hebrews 5:12 NLT. Like many of you, before coming here, "You have been believers so long now that you ought to be teaching others. Instead, you need someone to teach you again the basic things about God's word. You are like babies who need milk and cannot eat solid food [meat]."

Soon after, I began being spiritually fed for the first time—right after I read Erin's first book. Then, just like the verse says above, I did find myself able to teach others. As I began reading the praise reports and all the testimonies—even being fed by the many I had submitted myself and a few books I had personally written—I was no longer starving for the truth, and I began teaching more and more women.

When I asked for Him to enlighten me more, He went on to remind me of how important it was to give my praise and share testimonies and truths I'd learned, all due to my newly gained spiritual strength that I'd received. He said, by submitting praise and testimonies to be used, it was like I was donating my own blood for surgery, or bone marrow for my own transplant. By giving, encouragement would be ready for me when a crisis hit my own life. And I know I'm not alone. Many of you have experienced the very same thing, when you read your own praise report or testimony that is posted; it appears just when you (and others) need to hear it. Each bit of encouragement has fed you with an extra boost, when you were really struggling. It was just perfect, just what you needed to overcome what was about to destroy you.

Though you've probably heard it before from Erin, let's be sure you have one thing straight: God doesn't *need* your money! He owns everything. He is only providing you with an opportunity to **invest** into what He's doing! When you tithe, you are going to reap the blessings of every life that is changed! When you give to your storehouse, which is where God tells you to tithe, which is where you are fed, God allows you to share in all that the ministry or mission does: with *their* giving, *their* sowing, and *their* changing lives in your community or around the world. Giving to our storehouse is where we need to invest our money, instead of investing in stocks or property—whose sole purpose is to make more money, not do the work of the Lord. And what's even better news is that, even if a ministry or a mission falls, God will cover your losses and bless you with outrageous rewards (usually more than doubled) for your cheerful, giving heart!!

"Instead of your shame you will have a *double portion,* and instead of humiliation they will shout for joy over their portion. Therefore they will possess a *double portion* in their land, everlasting joy will be theirs" (Isaiah 61:7).

12. Teetering on the Brink of Prosperity 115

All this comes from tithing, along with His assurance for you to stop the devourer. "**Then** I will rebuke the devourer for you…" (Malachi 3:11).

After coming to terms with the act of tithing, still, many of you will then begin to struggle, wondering *where* you should tithe. Maybe you're a member of a church that you haven't gone to recently, or you have a church that you still tithe to (but no longer attend), or maybe you have recently been watching an encouraging television evangelist. To add to the confusion, you come daily to RMI to read the books for free, take the courses for free, and you are encouraged by real truth, each morning for free. So, now you are not sure *where* you should be tithing.

*By the way, tithing means 10% of your income: on the gross (or full amount). So, you can choose if you want to be blessed on the gross (or full amount) OR be blessed on the net (or your take home pay.) If you want to be blessed on the smaller amount (the net or your take home pay), guess what? God leaves that up to you, just like He does everything else. Yes, the choice is yours! You can choose to follow Him or decide that it is too great a price, so you turn and walk away from the opportunity.

Where **do you tithe?**

It's simple. You tithe where you are being fed, where you receive what you need to keep you going day after day. For me and for many of you, this means RMI. But for those of you who are primarily fed by your local church, tithe there, but that doesn't absolve you from giving to RMI or another ministry who also feeds you— no more than your primary grocery store or food club is the only place you *pay* for your groceries. If you go to a specialty gourmet store for the items that make your life a bit easier or more enjoyable, I don't think they would understand (nor should they) that you only faithfully pay your bill down the street where you are a food club member—not if you've been coming and taking from *their* storehouse!

Let me share something with you. About a year ago, a light came on when I went to Bible Gateway, and I realized that I had never given a thing to them, even though I go there regularly. So, I sought the Lord for an amount that I knew was past due, and even though it was a very large sum of money, I gave that donation amount—only to be enormously blessed almost immediately, receiving double. Isaiah 40:2, "Speak kindly . . . And call out to her, that her warfare has ended, that her iniquity has been removed, that she has received of the LORD'S hand DOUBLE for all her sins."

Soon after first writing this chapter, I realize that I needed to put Bible Gateway as one of my monthly auto-payments, just as I do with my tithe and other giving or offerings that the Lord has laid on my heart. When I did, I had to laugh. After I paused my writing to go to the site and set up an auto-donation (so I wouldn't forget), it brought me to the amount to give each month. So, like always, I asked Him, and He led me to put in a monthly amount that was almost three times the amount I had *planned* on giving them.

UPDATE: After donating a substantial amount each month as an offering to Bible Gateway for years, I discovered their donation button was gone. Then while searching their site, I read that they no longer accept donations. What a shame. Instead, it stated they'd begun to advertise. So, I asked Him for a way to pay. That's when He showed me two things. First, how I don't go to their site as I once had been doing. Instead, He led me to put all Erin's books, all my books and all the verses I used over and over again into one document that I can search. And should I not be able to find a verse, months before I began just Googling key words to discover the scripture reference. In other words, right when they stopped accepting donations, I'd stopped using their site as I once had. Like everything, His wonders never cease to keep me in a state of constant awe.

Secondly, though I do it nowhere else, He also led me to often click on some of the advertisements that they know I would be interested in. With the little I know, I do believe each click pays Bible Gateway a small amount. Again, I never even see the ads on other sites, and I've yet to click on them. This is only due to how I live. "He leads me" (Psalm 23) is how I live with my HH, walking hand in hand every waking moment. Yes, it's heaven.

Going Higher

Many of you have embraced the principle of tithing, but soon after you will be called to go higher. Maybe the truth is: all of us will be "called" to go higher, but only a brave few will *choose* to actually begin to make the climb. For me, my first major climb was immediately after my divorce, when I knew that I was facing financial ruin. I had been faithfully tithing, and so had my husband while we were married, but when he told me emphatically that we were about to lose our home (and probably right after the divorce), it was actually God calling me to go higher. Like all crises, this enormous crisis was His way of leading me toward a new path He wanted me to take.

Funny thing is, when I got the word from God on what to do, His solution is something my ex-husband tried to stop me from doing. God's solution, not surprisingly, was to GIVE. [By the way, if he had been my husband, of course I would have submitted without question. However, once divorced we do not submit to an ex-husband, no more than if he asked to sleep with him.] Also, as a way of teaching you a key principle, watch for increased opposition, when He's asked you to do something. It's a clear sign that what's up ahead is intended to bring about a tremendous reward. Just be certain it's not God who is trying to stop you from danger, like Balaam in Numbers 22:21-39.

Please remember too, it's human nature to want to pull back when we are faced with things that cause fear. Financial ruin causes fear. People reminding us of our "foolishness" causes fear. Nevertheless, I knew that without God I was completely ruined anyway, and therefore whatever He told me to do, I would do. So, He laid something HUGE on my heart, during a time when all the bills and financial commitments I already had were burying me. He chose to remind me of something that had been neglected, a pledge to the church we'd been attending, a pledge my husband and I both had made almost two years earlier.

*Many of you who read my prior book, *Poverty Mentality*, know my testimony. Yet each time I think about it, or share it, its message encourages me enormously. So, I hope you won't skip ahead and miss being strengthened, when I share this testimony again.

As a couple, we had made a pledge to our church for $10,000, and it had not been paid when he left me. Only a very small portion had been paid over the two years, and there were only 2 weeks until it was due, when the Lord reminded me about it. Here I was with the possibility of losing my home (which is what my ex-husband believed and why he, in the divorce he filed, had his attorney draft a judgment against me to get the equity in our home awarded to him, without the judge presiding over the divorce knowing about it).

Then, when the efforts of my ex-husband didn't work to stop me from paying the pledge (again, because he was no longer my husband, so I knew I couldn't submit to him), that's when he began rallying my children to try to stop me. Yet, I knew that all I had was the Lord, and without HIM I was ruined. Therefore, I had to follow and do what was right, no matter what.

Though fear tried to stop me, and doubt that I was doing the right thing plagued me, He showed me a way to pay what was due. I obeyed what He said and chose to pay the remainder of that pledge, and within only 2 HOURS, someone emailed me saying that they'd just written a check and they were sending me a check for $10,000—which was the full amount of the pledge—not just the portion I just had paid, but the entire amount!!

Now I know that the real blessing was not the money at all; it was the faith that He built in me that day. The blessings were the principles that God implanted in my heart that day. He had proved to me, through this crisis, that each time that you or I choose to do what God says—no matter what—even if met with opposition from others and from within us (feelings of fear and doubt that what you or I will do is the right thing) and we do it—magnificent blessings are on the other side just waiting for us. In addition, I learned that by telling my

HH I would do what He asked if He helped me, no matter what, **He** would make it happen, as I walked forward holding His hand.

Even though I didn't have the money to pay that pledge, no matter how hard I tried to find a way, along with the deadline for the pledge coming and going too, no matter how many times everyone tried to tell me that God did not expect me to pay it, and the church (if they knew my situation) would not expect me to pay it—God continued to urge me to trust Him and not pull back. And the result, again, was not just that huge amount of money, the full amount, being given back to me two hours later. Nor was it being told that I was right (by my ex-husband). No, the greatest benefit and gift was the FAITH that He built into me that day, faith that no one can ever take away. Also, I now have this powerful spiritual arsenal, my testimony, that I've given to countless others around the world.

Now, here I am again at that place where it looks like I am going to go under. Since there is much more at stake, the tests, understandably, are harder. His first test was asking me to choose to take the first fruits and sow them into lives that would be changed, rather than to pay my taxes. Reason and guilt (and maybe a bit of a "religious" spirit) made me feel I needed to pay the taxes first, because it looked (on paper) like I wouldn't have enough to pay my taxes. But as I spoke to my HH, the Lord, I knew the first fruits needed to be sown into what He was doing in the lives of so many who need Him. So, that's what I did.

Just two days later, AFTER I chose to resist fear or my religious spirit, I was informed by our state tax department to wait to see *if* I did indeed need to pay the taxes! They contacted me, informing me that they believed there was an error when I filed (my error, not theirs). Correcting my error meant that I owed nothing, in the exact same way my federal taxes turned out. My mistake in my federal taxes was what led them to give me a refund that ended up as a direct deposit in my bank account, my first fruits, which was the exact amount needed for my daughter's ticket and documentation to go to Africa. Each time, by making a "mistake," God had set it up so I would have money ready when I needed it.

*The term "first fruits" means that we give the first portion of what we get back to God. It's like giving your first-born son to God, as Samuel's mother did, only to be blessed with more children. In my situation, my income had totally dried up, with just a trickle coming in, when I got this very large and unexpected check for overpayment of my taxes, which they said was due to an error when I did my taxes myself. Even though no one found an error, when all was said and done, nevertheless, the money was there and ready.

So, even **if** we make a mistake, God is right there with this promise, "And we know that God causes all things to work together for good to those who love God, to those who are called according to His purpose" (Romans 8:28). This promise and principle, alone, should always be used to help us move ahead, when we are too afraid to move forward—all we have to do is utilize its power by acting on it.

Gosh, what if we get lost, though, and lose our way? Not surprisingly, our HH has that concern covered too! "What man among you, if he has a hundred sheep and has lost one of them, does not leave the ninety-nine in the open pasture and go after the one which is lost until he finds it?" (Luke 15:4). Though this verse is key for salvation, it also is a principle that works when you or I get lost, or feel we are. I know.

Though sowing those first fruits was difficult, to say the least, the second test, which I believe is what I hope to be my "finals," makes the first pale in comparison. All through my journey of moving my mountain of debt, I have told God and anyone who would listen that it would be GOD who would supply all my needs!

Desperate to make it happen MY WAY, as I said, I neglected fully teaching the principle of tithing, primarily sharing that RMI was my storehouse and was probably yours too. Then, I realized it was somewhat purposefully that I did it, when I realized that each time I was prompted, I was afraid women who have felt led to donate to my ministry (or to RMI where I am paid) would give to their storehouse—when I wanted it to come straight from God! Doesn't the way we think often make you question your sanity? Hmmm, well, maybe it's just me.

12. Teetering on the Brink of Prosperity

Knowing full well that when anyone fails to give when and where she should, she soon would come up lacking or short on funds, I continued to resist encouraging all of you to make sure YOU tithe and YOU give to *your* storehouse—no matter where it is. Honestly, I didn't consciously know I was doing it—until the Lord opened my eyes to what was/is happening to so many of my close friends, women I minister to. Once I realized this truth, I came to the crossroads that would determine my future and yours. What was I going to do now?

By telling many of you that you have failed to GIVE to your storehouse (which means there is not going to be food enough, nor even a storehouse), it will certainly mean that many will judge my motives and conclude that I am using you to make my own mountain fall. People are quick to judge. Yet honestly, my struggles go even deeper than what *you* may think of me. My greatest and deepest struggle is that I didn't want it this way! I wanted, and asked God again and again, to bring my resources from outside the ministry (not through increased donations or more book sales by adding a new book). Instead, I wanted to give to RMI and give to others, needing nothing from anyone other than from God!!

Then, just the other day, God reminded me of how I told Him how I wanted all His promises to me to be done prior to writing *Finding the Abundant Life*. I wanted Him to change and radically transform my husband (so that we could minister together as a couple) and hoped that God would give him the same passion that I had, something that he lacked. Instead, He chose to remove him—the most scandalous and hardest way He could have brought about His promises!!

"'For My thoughts are not your thoughts, nor are your ways My ways,' declares the LORD. 'For as the heavens are higher than the earth, so are My ways higher than your ways and My thoughts than your thoughts'" (Isaiah 55:8–9).

Right now, I know that if I don't tell many of you that you have been robbing God (Malachi 3:8–10), because you have not faithfully tithed to your *storehouse*, I know you will go under financially. Though this is probably the hardest decision I have ever had to make as a minister of His truths, I am washed up anyway if I don't choose to step out and obey the Lord. "Why do you call Me, 'Lord, Lord,' and do not do what I say?" (Luke 6:46). Instead, I must risk being thought of as trying to get your money and making my own mountain fall myself, by my pressing you to give.

However, whether or not *you* give is not the determining factor, but whether or not I will do what He has called me to do— will I speak the truth no matter what you or anyone else thinks? Asking you to give is what everyone has been telling me to do, but I didn't want to do it. And when I have taken this to the Lord, He has reminded me of two other chapters, where I wrestled with Him all night, not wanting to write what I have revealed to everyone. But I did, no matter what anyone thought, including how I thought about myself. By far, I have been my greatest opposition in all of this; I really see it now for the first time, at least the magnitude of this "self" that is just struggling to stay alive when I want the self in me to die. I just hope and pray and plead with God that by doing what is right, no matter what, it will mean that that the SELF *will* die.

Here is what I know: if I do what is right, God will make my mountain come down, and He is going to choose how to do it. The point is this—and it's what I have said all along—it will be GOD who supplies all my needs (not you, not my books, not a pay raise: not by donations or book sales). It's not going to depend upon my ability to get my point across or even how accurately and deeply I share my heart with you. It will all depend upon God's faithfulness to His word, when we trust Him, and we prove so by our actions.

"But someone may well say, 'You have faith and I have works; show me your faith without the works, and I will show you my faith *by my works"* (James 2:18).

Chapter 13

A Purse with Holes

> "You have sown much, but harvest little;
> You eat, but there is not enough to be satisfied;
> You drink, but there is not enough to become drunk;
> You put on clothing, but no one is warm enough;
> And he who earns, earns wages
> to put into a **purse with holes**."
> —Haggai 1:6

It's been several weeks since I wrote and posted the last chapter. Looking back, I have to laugh at my childlike faith. Immediately after posting it, I began looking for that "six-figure check" in the mailbox, in my post office box, or in an email from someone telling me it was on its way. That's the way it happened last time, the last two times, as a matter of fact, huge checks just showed up—immediately after I radically obeyed, but not this time.

So sure that everything would happen instantaneously, I had the last chapter of the book titled quite appropriately "Mountain Moved" just sitting there ready and waiting for my fantastic testimony. A testimony that would leave everyone speechless, in awe, dumbfounded.

When it didn't happen by the end of the week, I wasn't sure what to do, so I began posting testimonies from other women who had seen mountains move in their lives. Some were quite good, a couple amazing, some were just so-so (at least for the reader; sort of "you had to have been there" quality). But they filled the gap until I could write and post *my* testimony—my mountain moved; that huge mountain of debt, gone, vanished, and sitting deep at the bottom of the sea.

After a few weeks had passed, I figured I needed to switch gears into the "waiting" principle. You know, so I would be ready with the "mount up with wings as eagles" variety. Isaiah 40:31 KJV, "But they that wait upon the LORD shall renew their strength; they shall mount up with wings as eagles; they shall run, and not be weary; and they shall walk, and not faint." I mean, that's a lot of money and responsibility to carry, so waiting, I decided, would get me all pumped up spiritually, or so I thought. I began to work on other projects to busy myself, while I waited for my miracle to break open and to see the showers of blessings pour over my life.

Looking back, I am not sure how many weeks into this period of waiting that, what "broke" was not my miracle, but a startling revelation that took me completely by surprise.

Due to writing this book and posting it, I discovered a much deeper understanding of giving and the need to give. As a result, many fellow RMI members also became convicted and started to give too. They began to tithe to RMI and then send their offering to me. As soon as the checks began to pour in, I thought that maybe there wouldn't be just one big check, but hundreds (maybe thousands) of small checks and online donations whereby that would provide my amazing testimony. The women who sent them, almost immediately, became "My Heroes."

Rather than send the usual automated response, I began sending out personal thank you notes and also asking everyone to explain how He'd been showing them other things about tithing. Without realizing it, God was about to use several fellow RMI members to teach me, and the very first lesson was a doozy.

Early one morning I got a really nice email from a close friend and RMI member in Europe, but there was something she said that I just couldn't shake. This precious member mentioned, in the course of her testimony, about a ministry that was struggling, so she asked them if *they* were tithing.

13. A Purse with Holes

It was early in the morning, as I said, so I just read right over this point since I *knew* "I" was tithing. Erin was tithing. And RMI was always "tithing" by giving books away for free online. I'd learned how RMI send out free books when someone couldn't afford a book. Even noting that Encouraging Bookstore "tithed" when they'd send out books when someone's credit card was declined. Yet, all of a sudden, I understood—that wasn't really "tithing"!

My beliefs on tithing were first challenged when my husband ATT (at the time) was still in full-time ministry. Often, he got very upset with me because he said I made him debate this issue of tithing. To be honest, we really never debated at all. The truth was that he knew I felt convicted that we should tithe from everything: the sale of our books and from donations received, and he felt we shouldn't. So, as a wise woman wannabe, I no longer involved myself in anything financial while married, after studying *A Wise Woman*. Yet just knowing how I felt made him angry with me. Often, without saying a word, my husband ATT would go into rants on this topic but as taught, I remain quiet simply nodding my head.

Then, one evening I found myself in a position to actually ask the pastor who ran the finances of the megachurch where we attended at the time; a church that was very blessed and debt free!! Normally I would never ever ask anyone, anything, "Let the woman keep silent in the churches. If they desire to learn anything, let them ask their *own* husbands at home; for it is improper for a woman to speak in church." 1 Corinthians 14:34-35. Yet, I had the strongest sense that what I felt "convicted of" may be guilt.

That night this pastor told me that small ministries such as ours really couldn't afford to tithe or they would go under. He said that tithing should only be paid from our "personal" income—not 10% from our ministry. He convinced me that to also give from our ministry income was "double tithing" since we were basically a sole proprietorship. After being enlightened, I was eager to get back home in order to humble myself and tell my husband ATT that he was right, and I was wrong. "Most gladly therefore, I will rather boast about my weaknesses, that the power of Christ may dwell in me.

Therefore I am well content with weaknesses, with insults, with distresses, with persecutions, with difficulties, for Christ's sake; for when I am weak, then I am strong." Philippians 12:9-10.

So now, years later is when I read the testimony about the other ministries' financial woes and the source, which was that they were **not** tithing as a ministry. That's when I had to take a long hard look at what I had been told, even if it was from someone I admired, and assumed would certainly know the truth regarding ministries and churches tithing.

Thankfully, God knew my heart and He knows that I continually and will forever crave for His truth! It's not just about me (nor is it just about you either); my family and my members are counting on me to seek the truth and live by the truth—no matter what. So, I kept seeking and asking the Lord to show me the truth. Wow, did He ever.

First, He reminded me that this pastor was no longer running or handled the finances of this megachurch. Several years later someone wanted to tell me details, saying he'd been asked to leave our megachurch and was not welcomed elsewhere. They said that something wasn't "right" and wanted to share more; however, I asked this person not to tell me why or any details. It really didn't matter to me why he left, and I also didn't want to be in a place where I judged him, lest I be judged. Yet, it did make me wonder if this misinformation had finally led to his disastrous outcome (see James 3:1).

Leaving that thought behind, the Lord then reminded me of a huge ministry that was *more* than prospering. I knew that they tithed from everything they received as a donation, so much so, that they were able to help support lesser ministries as the Lord led them. This proved to be so prosperous that they actually had to start new ministries of their own, each was fed from the 10% the main ministry took in.

Right away, I knew I wanted to do that too!!! I wanted it for my ministry and also for RMI to be in that place! I shared all of this with Erin, who I knew would be just as excited, and of course, she was!!

13. A Purse with Holes   127

That's when it hit me—why would a ministry or church "go under" if they tithed?? That seemed so ludicrous the minute I really thought about it! Isn't that what people think about tithing? All tithing?

So why, then, would God have allowed me to run into that pastor, at that particular time, if what he told me was not true? To keep the peace. My husband ATT was *seeking* to be set free from the law of tithing, and what you seek is what you will find. (Matthew 7:7) God also used the situation to, once again, train me for deeper submission to an earthly husband so that I would be ready to be the bride of my now, Heavenly Husband.

Also, by excitedly humbling myself and telling my husband ATT that I was wrong, and then abiding by what I had been told, prepared me for much greater acts of submission. It was just two weeks after my divorce when I was packing my bags and traveling around the world; traveling, something I loathed more than anything I can think of right now.

I also believe that it was God "setting me up."

Though most Christians seem to love to give the devil credit for every crisis in their lives, the Bible actually tells us in Isaiah 45:6–7 "That men may know from the rising to the setting of the sun That there is no one besides Me. I am the LORD, and there is no other, The One forming light and creating darkness, causing well-being and **creating calamity;** I am the LORD who does all these."

Just as He set up the Israelites with huge adversities that allowed them to flee the Egyptian bondage so they could set off to The Promised Land. God set me up way back then so that I could see and experience firsthand the consequences of failing to tithe by "going into exile for [my] lack of knowledge" (Isaiah 5:13). God allows each of us places of exile— not so we panic and think God has forsaken us—because He can't! Isaiah 49:15 "Can a woman forget her nursing child and have no compassion on the son of her womb? Even these may forget, but I will not forget you."

No, the Lord uses our times of exile and drought in order that we might experience Him to the fullest.

As we obey and seek Him, our sorrow is soon turned into dancing! (Psalm 30:11) Even though I truly believed I would be dancing due to the six-figure check that I would receive, I found myself dancing when I was able to tithe from my own ministry, likewise, Erin began rigorously tithing throughout each of RMI's ministries.

All I can say is—giving— in the midst of my lack— felt marvelous!!

The next thing the Lord reminded me was when I got my very first BIG donation, just two and a half weeks from my divorce—I tithed from it! And I was thrilled to do so too!!! I remember feeling led to give to a couple of African ministries, one that built churches, something I had *longed* to do for years but something my husband ATT would never consider doing.

That is when I realized that I could NOT remember ever tithing on the next BIG donation, and it was years ago. Yet, the next revelation was that God didn't say just to tithe on our HUGE increases, but on EVERYTHING!! So, then, I knew I needed to know how I was going to pay all those back tithes, and *where* He wanted me to tithe.

I knew it was God who had to show me the way. I was nervous and excited to set out on a new journey and chapter of my life! This is the verse He gave me that I read over and over and over again for days until it was time.

Caught Up with Taking Care of Your Own Houses

Haggai 1:3–11 MSG

"How is it that it's the 'right time' for you to live in your fine new homes while the Home, God's Temple, is in ruins?" [asked God].

"Take a good, hard look at your life. Think it over. You have spent a lot of money, but you haven't much to show for it.

You keep filling your plates, but you never get filled up.

You keep drinking and drinking and drinking, but you're always thirsty.

You put on layer after layer of clothes, but you can't get warm. And the people who work for you, what are they getting out of it? Not much—a leaky, rusted-out bucket, that's what.

"Take a good, hard look at your life. Think it over."

Then God said: "Here's what I want you to do… rebuild the Temple. Do it just for Me. Honor me. You've had great ambitions for yourselves, but nothing has come of it. The little you have brought to my Temple I've blown away—there was nothing to it.

"And why?"

"Because while you've run around, caught up with taking care of your own houses, my Home is in ruins. That's why."

"Because of your stinginess."

"And so, I've given you a dry summer and a skimpy crop. I've matched your tight-fisted stinginess by decreeing a season of drought, drying up fields and hills, withering gardens and orchards, stunting vegetables and fruit. Nothing—not man or woman, not animal or crop—is going to thrive."

Selah. Stop and think about that for a while!!

Chapter 14

Eaten Alive

"Then I will rebuke the devourer for you."
—Malachi 3:11

Once the Lord revealed the huge gap in the wall of my finances, due to my lack of ministry tithing, I began to notice that all the frustrations that I had been experiencing were due to the "devourer" coming in and taking what was rightfully his to take!

We can ignore it, but the fact is that God says that we are to "'Bring the whole tithe into the storehouse, so that there may be food in My house, and test Me now in this,' says the LORD of hosts, 'if I will not open for you the windows of heaven and pour out for you a blessing until it overflows. *Then* I will rebuke the devourer for you, so that it will not destroy the fruits of the ground; nor will your vine in the field cast its grapes,' says the LORD of hosts" Malachi 3:10-12.

It seemed that everything I owned, all of a sudden, was in ill-repair or broken: a computer, our front porch lights, our kitchen table, our water cooler, our dishwasher, our kitchen water filter, and many more things that I can't remember right now. The devourer also came in and rightfully stole from us, something dear to me—pictures on my laptop, which included all the pictures from our four years on our farm, and later, my around the world travel pictures—they were all gone.

It came to a peak when, in just one day, my daughter, bless her heart, broke the window shade in my bedroom and within minutes had taken the finish off the ceiling fan in our living room. That's when I realized—we were being EATEN ALIVE!!

My Heavenly Husband was so patient, good, gracious, and loving (as usual) as He led me through past checks to confirm what He had laid on my heart—that I had not tithed from the second huge donation to our ministry. Then He showed me that is when all my books in my warehouse and ministry office had been destroyed. And not surprisingly, that's when I realized that my lack of funds was all part of the consequences of my lack of knowledge because God said, "my people are destroyed from lack of knowledge" Hosea 4:6.

And yet, do I even need to tell you how **good** and **gracious** God is?!?

Just knowing that I needed to pay my ministry's past tithes did not result in automatically being able to pay them. You might be thinking, "Well, of course, since you are in a financial crisis, how could you pay them?!" But that was really not the problem at all. From the moment that I set my heart to tithe, I found so many things that began blocking me!

It began with the first back tithe I owed. The Lord showed me would send a missionary to Africa. However, suddenly, at the last minute, she had no place to stay, so we waited; waiting a total of twelve weeks. In the meantime, all I could do was think about how (without that tithe paid) the devourer would continue to wreak havoc in our home.

Some people who knew about what was going on told me to simply pay it elsewhere; I mean, why not? The reason is simple: when God tells you to do something specific you should never deviate from it. And I will let you in on a little secret that will help you—be prepared for people coming out of nowhere to try to get you to change the path He's leading you on. This is nothing new, we see it in the book of First Samuel 15:22–24 when it says…

"Behold, to **obey is better than sacrifice,** and to heed than the fat of rams. For rebellion is as the sin of divination, and insubordination is as iniquity and idolatry. Because you have rejected the Word of the Lord, He has also rejected you from being king. Then Saul said to Samuel, 'I have sinned; I have indeed transgressed the command of the LORD and your words, because I feared the people and *listened to their voice.*'"

Some people take this lightly, I don't. I have chosen to live by each principle He's revealed to me and it has cost me. Yet, whatever I have lost I have gained ten-fold. Most of what I have lost is my reputation and my friends. People tend to think you are crazy when you follow the Lord without question. Saul did and it cost him his crown.

Of course, I wanted to buy her ticket so I could be on my way to correcting my "back tithe" situation, but there was nothing I could do until the doors opened again for Africa. To pay it somewhere else would be to open myself (and my ministry) to destruction.

If you think for one moment that I would risk **everything** by trying to stray from the Lord's leading, you haven't read enough of my books. Besides, I have learned the secret of this well-known yet dreaded "waiting period." Watching what happened, as a result, this particular wait will be forever engraved in my mind to help me see the future, past the wait, to what is waiting for me on the other side (but that, dear reader you will have to wait to read in a future chapter).

It was during the wait that the Lord began to gently show me that I needed to begin fixing my "back" tithe situation by paying "current" tithes. A no-brainer for you, perhaps, but for me, it was an exciting revelation! At that point, I felt my Heavenly Husband say that the last batch of the donations needed to be tithed to where the missionary would be going, an orphanage for AIDS babies in South Africa.

Yet, when I attempted to give there, I found that they were in the process of getting their new site up! Just trying to do what was right brought about nothing but delays, one after another! Sound familiar? So many Christians think that once they get past the hurdle of fighting their flesh to do what is right, that the rest comes easily. It may for a baby Christian, but for most of us, setting off to do what God has called us to do is just the beginning of the battle. Therefore, don't give up, or worse—believe it wasn't God's will after all; that somehow you missed God. If you want to do great things for God, then when opposition comes against you it is a sign that you are on the right path after all.

Though I was being stopped, the greatest mystery is—God *always* and will forever see the *intent* and *desires* of our hearts. Did you know that? Isn't His grace just beyond comprehension sometimes? Even though I hadn't paid a single back tithe or even a single current tithe, things in my home and my life began to improve. Not because I performed the proper "task or duty," but just because, as always, He looks at our heart "for man **looks** at the outward appearance, but the LORD **looks** at the **heart**" (1 Samuel 16:7).

"For by grace you have been saved through faith; and that not of yourselves, it is the gift of God; not as a result of works, so that no one may boast" (Ephesians 2:8–10).

Getting my back tithes caught up and paid, I experienced each and every day that they were, for me, impossible. And that dear reader was really great news! Do you know why? For "Behold, I am the LORD, the God of all flesh; is anything too difficult for **Me**?" (Jeremiah 32:27). To which I love to shout...

"Ah Lord GOD! Behold, You have made the heavens and the earth by Your great power and by Your outstretched arm! Nothing is too difficult for **You**"! (Jeremiah 32:17).

Finances and Salvation

Now let me take this to a higher plane. In the Bible, God always compares our finances to salvation. That means that in the same way I am *unable* to pay my debt for my sins, He allowed me to see that I am totally *unable* to pay my debts, which now included back, or past tithes owed to Him.

Just as it would be foolish for me to set out on a journey to pay for my past sins, it also would be foolish for me to try to pay my debt, owed to Him, for past tithes.

The Lord then encouraged me (which means that He *gave me* courage) by using one of my own testimonies. He reminded me of the first task after my divorce that He laid on my heart with the building pledge that my husband ATT (at the time) had not paid. The Lord didn't put that on my heart as a burden, but as a blessing—as I watched *Him* provide the thousands not yet paid. I knew I couldn't do it, but God could, and He did within a two-week period. Impossible? Yes, but once again, nothing, not one thing, is impossible with God.

We read in Romans 13:8 that it tells us to "Owe nothing to anyone except to **love** one another."

How could the Lord tell us something that would cause a burden on us, when He came to be our Burden-Bearer? When He tells us to owe no man, so that we are free to just love them, it is *not* a burden, but a blessing! Because *He* provided the means to pay that debt (as we look to Him for it) as well as the love that we are to love others with!! What could be more beautiful?!

The question I had to ask though was "Why?" Why did I miss this? Why didn't I know (been enlightened, had a revelation) to tithe from the ministry when I first took over the ministry? The answer is because God does create calamity. "The One forming light and creating darkness, causing well-being and **creating calamity;** I am the LORD who does all these" (Isaiah 45:7).

God creates calamity in our lives, not so we can feel abandoned, ashamed, or so we can work our way out of it, but so He can prove to others, through our lives, that He is there for us and will see us *through* when others believe we're through!! Can you shout, "Thank You, Lord!"?

God created calamity in the lives of so many of our Bible heroes; just sit for a moment and think about it. If Israel had not been in the calamity of bondage, the Israelites would have never seen the power and compassion of God; therefore, there would have been no need for Moses or his brother Aaron. Where would you and I be without the testimony of the Red Sea? Being fed with manna? And, after years of wandering, where would we be without the testimony of the Israelites finally crossing the Jordan into the Promised Land?

Being in a place like this, then, should be exciting and not frightening at all!

How many of you are in this place? I believe a lot of you are.

If you are like me, you've been stealing from God by not tithing, and suddenly this is a revelation to you. And, getting it paid may seem like the impossible dream—but God makes a way when there seems no way. All you have to do is *give it* to Him again, and again, and again!

That's what I have done, and in the next chapter, I will share with you this portion of my life-changing journey.

Update: Years after this chapter was written, the pictures from our four years on our farm and my world travel pictures—suddenly were recovered. Without looking, without complaining, suddenly, they were back.

Chapter 15
Rebuild the Temple

> "**Rebuild** the temple,
> that I may be pleased with it and be glorified,'
> says the LORD."
> —Haggai 1:8

Let me begin this chapter with a bit of encouragement, by sharing my first step toward looking to the Lord for His plan of getting my past/back tithes paid. As I gave it to Him again, and again, and again, I found that the first step was to get excited, rather than panic, and actually **boast** about my weaknesses. For, "He has said to me, 'My grace is sufficient for you, for power is perfected in weakness.' Most gladly, therefore, I will rather boast about my weaknesses, so that the power of Christ may dwell in me" (2 Corinthians 12:9).

Knowing I needed His power to dwell in me, big time, instead of sharing this with all my children at once, I took the time to share it with each of them alone. I also made a point of sharing my weaknesses, how I had failed to pay tithes, with some of my closest friends. I was ecstatic to find several opportunities that God opened up for me to share this with acquaintances and even some strangers. I knew that this boasting would give me the power I needed to press forward with the upcoming challenges I was about to face, which would ultimately change the course of my life.

The next step was to seek God for how to start. He showed me that I needed to begin with the first tithe I failed to pay, the largest one, which meant I had to tithe more than a thousand dollars "somewhere", as I mentioned earlier in this chapter. Trust me, this amount seemed like a lot, especially because I had recently gotten several bank overdraft notices. Yet, this is how it usually happens.

15. Rebuild the Temple

God loves to stack the odds, raise the impossibilities. So, here I was with no money in my accounts as I tried to hang on. In addition, I just got a notice that a new credit card had turned me down (a credit card I didn't even want or apply for but what was sent to me)—that's when I fully realized that God was just making a point!

And maybe you're thinking, as I was, how could she have so many people (my wonderful "heroes" as I call them) who have been donating to her ministry, but her bank account is just barely staying open? How is this even possible?

Because, remember, my purse has holes in it!!

"Now therefore, thus says the LORD of hosts, 'Consider your ways!

You have sown much, but harvest little; you eat, but there is not enough to be satisfied; you drink, but there is not enough to become drunk; you put on clothing, but no one is warm enough; and he who earns, earns wages to put into *a purse with holes.* Thus says the LORD of hosts, 'Consider your ways!

Go up to the mountains, bring wood and *rebuild the temple,* that I may be pleased with it and be glorified,' says the LORD.

'You look for much, but behold, it comes to little; when you bring it home, I blow it away Why?' declares the LORD of hosts, 'Because of My house which lies desolate, while each of you runs to his own house.'" (Haggai 1:5-9).

And if a purse with holes was not enough of a problem, add to this that the wall to my finances and my life has a huge gap in it!!

"I searched for a man among them who would build up the wall and stand in the **gap** before Me for the land, so that I would not destroy it; but I found no one" (Ezekiel 22:30).

All I wanted to do was immediately sew up the hole in my purse and patch up that gaping space in my wall—but I had no money to buy mortar or a needle and thread!

What are you and I supposed to do?

Isaiah 55:1-3 The Free Offer of Mercy

"Ho! Every one who thirsts, come to the waters;

And you who have no money come, buy and eat

Come, buy wine and milk

Without money and without cost.

"Why do you spend money for what is not bread,

And your wages for what does not satisfy?

Listen carefully to Me, and eat what is good,

And delight yourself in abundance.

"Incline your ear and come to Me

Listen, that you may live;

And I will make an everlasting covenant with you,

According to the faithful mercies shown to David."

Darling, are you where I am too? And, wow, do you see? There is no fear. All we have to do is relax and *give it* to our Heavenly Husband to work out for us. He's got the perfect plan— so why do we waste our time and effort by trying to think of our own plan that wears us out, worries us to death, until we give up—so we will *finally* turn everything over to Him?

"'For My thoughts are not your thoughts, nor are your ways My ways,' declares the LORD. 'For as the heavens are higher than the earth, so are My ways higher than your ways and My thoughts than your thoughts'" (Isaiah 55:8–9).

"'For I know the plans that I have for you,' declares the LORD, 'plans for welfare and not for calamity to give you a **future** and a **hope**'" (Jeremiah 29:11).

15. Rebuild the Temple

My Heavenly Husband was way ahead of me (duh). Remember that tax return that I sowed as my "first fruits"? Well, guess what? Though I had planned to use it to help send RMI's first missionary to Africa, due to the hole in my purse, a series of "autopayments" in my checking account had used it up. Suddenly, when I looked, if I had to help at that *exact moment,* I wouldn't have had enough!

That's what happens when we figure out a plan, doesn't it? However, when we look to Him, and not ourselves, that's when we find we are never short. The very day I saw this dilemma, I felt led to go out to my mailbox, and on my way there, I kept telling Him that I didn't want to open it because *that* mailbox only brought me bills, overdraft notices, and cruel letters.

But, then, when I opened it, there it was—another government tax refund! How could it be? Believe it or not, I opened the envelope and received **double** just like He said I would!

"Speak kindly to Jerusalem; and call out to her, that her warfare has ended, that her iniquity has been removed, that she has received of the LORD'S hand **Double** for all her **sins**" (Isaiah 40:2).

No one could understand how I could possibly get a second refund check, and surely there must be some sort of logical explanation. After some time had passed, I thought that our government tax offices must have made a mistake and so I was going to find out what I needed to do to send the check back. Yet, God graciously spoke truth to me through my son, when he said, "Mom, what are the chances of you being right versus the government being right? Taxes are their job, they are experts, right? You did your own taxes, obviously, the error is on your side" and happily in my favor!

Well, there you go! The first back tithe was paid and used to send a missionary to Africa after all. I couldn't wait to send the money for the ticket and began to shudder thinking that I needed to do it *fast* before anything else broke or we went completely under financially! Yet, God is never in a hurry, and He wants us to live hurry-free too.

Dearest bride, would you believe that just knowing the **intent** of my heart, all of a sudden, things that were broken *God* began repairing and replacing!?!

All of a sudden, my son fixed our kitchen table so now it is level and is sturdier than before. And my younger son watched as the Lord gave us immeasurable favor when he brought our broken water cooler to the store, and they gave us a brand-new cooler! And if that were not enough, as a man shopping showed up to get the cooler off the shelf and then another man showed up in the parking lot to put it in my car! If that were not amazing enough, when I purchased the first water cooler, it would *not* fit in my car. Yet, the replacement cooler slid right in even though they were both exactly the same size, the very same water cooler!

Other things that were broken began turning out to be blessings. Why? Because we have and can believe His promise, that I call my never-ending "get out of jail cards." First is Romans 8:28 "And we know that God causes all things to work together for good to those who love God, to those who are called according to His purpose."

Better yet, do what I do and take one of my favorite promises found in Isaiah 40:2 that we already read. Read it again and again until it becomes yours! "Speak kindly to Jerusalem; and call out to her, that her warfare has ended, that her iniquity has been removed, that she has received of the **Lord's** hand **double** for all her sins."

God's grace and mercy are there for us, and our Beloved died so we could have them. So why then do we not use what He died to give us? Does it make me want to sin or mess up? No, of course not. Actually, the opposite is true. Having His grace and mercy motivates me to live free from evil. Evil will only keep me bound and unable to love or give what He has died to give to you and me!

What God has already done confirms that He already has a plan to help me pay all my back tithes. And my back tithes are not just from the big donations I failed to tithe, but from all my ministry's increase.

In my finite and simple mind, of course, I have no idea *how* He is going to do it. Even if I gave everything I received somewhere, it means that I am still 10% short. So, do I give 90% plus 10%? And if I do, how can I pay my bills and not go under? Confused? I am.

But, guess what? I don't have to understand or know any of the details. All I have to do is look to Him. "They looked to Him and were radiant, and their faces will never be ashamed" (Psalm 34:5). "But seek first His kingdom and His righteousness, and **all these things** *will be added to you"* (Matthew 6:33).

Isn't that comforting? Isn't this freeing? Isn't this just too good to be true?! A lot like salvation isn't it?

Just be sure you encourage someone today with this message — so many need to hear it.

Clarification. We all learned in Erin's books that our tithe is given to our storehouse, Malachi 3:8–10, and our offering can be used as He leads Haggai 1:9. This is also true when it comes to our ministry's tithe. Though my personal tithe always goes to RMI, my ministry tithe is often sent and used elsewhere.

Chapter 16

Giving Frenzy

"Never shall You wash my feet!"
"Lord, then wash not only my feet,
But also my hands and my head"!
—John 13:7–9

Over the past few years, well actually, I suppose I realized it soon after my divorce. I began to notice that I am a lot like Peter of whom this opening verse is about.

Peter was one of the apostles who witnessed Jesus walking on water and believed He was a ghost. Then unlike the other apostles when Peter realized it was Jesus, he immediately jumped out of the boat to walk toward Him. Unfortunately, he was also the one who looked around at the wind and the waves and immediately began to sink. Thankfully, he also holds onto no pride and proceeded to cry out for Jesus to save him.

You'd think he would learn, but we saw this kind of behavior several times from him again, like this one in our opening verse, which occurred at the beginning of the Last Supper festivities. Peter was quick to try to stop Jesus from washing his feet (knowing the kind of sinner he was), but when Jesus told Peter that without allowing it, "you have no part with Me" Peter goes overboard, again, and asked Jesus to wash his hands, feet, and head!

Since I am comparing myself to this interesting fellow Peter, I think I would like to stop right here before I have to be reminded that Peter was the one who was absolutely sure that he would stand by Jesus, who he later denied…okay, let's stop right there. Or, better yet, let's fast forward to remind ourselves (this is more for *my* benefit than yours that Jesus did mention that after His resurrection, in Matthew 16:18, "I also say to you that you are Peter, and upon this Rock I will build My church; and the gates of Hades will not overpower it." Okay, that's better...

So, here's how I'm like Peter. When the Lord showed me that my financial woes were due to unpaid back tithes that had caused not only my "state of poverty," but also my children and my ministry's "death"... Okay, wait, before I go on, although I do believe that humility is always in vogue, in fashion as a believer, I don't want to paint the wrong picture of my circumstances. Let me rewind or regress just a bit...

Due to the fact that I had been tithing to my storehouse along with giving an offering that equaled 50% of my personal income, and though we had no huge bank account, and we did have debt coming out of our (my) ears, we were never lacking in *anything*. Nothing at all.

A lot of our living comfortably was due to the fact that the Lord had me write and live the principles in Breaking free from *The Poverty Mentality*. So, I was not violating any of those principles by stating "We can't afford it" nor was I thinking it either. From the moment of my divorce, I was free to break loose from all restraints—I was a woman on a mission to radically obey God no matter what!

And so, being the zealot that I am, when I met a medical missionary on a flight who got my attention when he told me about a man he knew who had given God 90% of his income, which is when I began to ask my Husband to help me to increase to that amount too— I just knew God had me sit beside this young man because that message was for me! And a few months later I had gotten up to giving 50% of my income. Yet none of this was what I was doing with my *ministry* income. Now, fast forwarding to the present...

At first, when I would think of the enormous amount of "back" tithes I knew I owed from my ministry income, the thought wanted to engulf me with horror and fear. That's when I chose to turn it around and focus on the fact that tithing means giving, and with so much in back tithes, there had to be *a lot of giving* up ahead. And to confirm this giving was in my future, I instantly remembered something I saved from a fortune cookie that said, "In your latter years you will be a philanthropist." If you don't know what a philanthropist is, you are not alone, it was only a few years earlier that I finally looked it up. Oh, I had heard the word but didn't exactly know what it meant.

So here is the official definition: philanthropist, wealthy people who give substantial amounts of money to support charitable, educational, or cultural institutions or activities; a desire to improve the material, social, and spiritual welfare of humanity, especially through charitable activities; general love for, or benevolence toward, the whole of humankind.

Sounds just like Jesus, doesn't it?

And would you believe, just the day before, the day **before** I opened that fortune cookie, I had asked God, "Make me a philanthropist"?

Before going on, I believe that there are a few of you that we have left behind. You are still staring in disbelief that I not only read a fortune cookie, but that I saved it, *and* believed God sent me that message in answer to my prayer.

Darling, if this is you, God doesn't really care about religious things like this; did you know that? Remember all the issues He has with the churches in Revelation? Yet if you read it, you will find that His focus was that their heart was to impress others with their "good works" that led to them leaving their first Love!

Once you know, and embrace your first Love, your Precious Heavenly Husband, and experience His love, you know that all that matters to Him is also all that should matter to you—being His and His alone. And when you are in His and His alone, you no longer live under the law, but you are free from the law so that you actually soar right over it. Honestly, it is hard to explain to someone who has never experienced this, and because this is not what this chapter is supposed to be about, I will have to move on. But, if I have gotten your attention, and you want to know how to live like this, then read or reread *Finding the Abundant Life* and then *Living the Abundant Life*. Both these books and all my books are free as courses on RMI's LoveAtLast.org ministry. Just another way to give.

Now, to get us back on track, where was I? Oh, I had just said that when I began thinking of how much my back tithes would be, at first, they wanted to engulf me with horror and fear; however, I *chose* to turn it around and focus on *all* the giving that was up ahead. And boy, did I get excited!!!

This began a giving frenzy!

Though God had transformed me into a giver years ago, after this revelation, I was almost out of control, but I was loving every part of it!

Giving became my passion. I gave big things, little things: time, money, and many of my possessions. If I had it, I gave it away. I gave to family, friends, enemies, and strangers.

Yet there was something I had that I didn't know was holding me back. Something that was keeping me in bondage. Something that prevents us all from experiencing the freedom of a most precious kind. And a lot of it was founded on my giving frenzy.

Most of us are not comfortable with *receiving*.

The majority of Christians are only comfortable with giving, and I was no exception. Yet the Bible tells us many times, specifically and theoretically, that we need to be able to do both, to be well-balanced, smack dab in the center of the narrow road, such as we see in the life of the apostle, Paul.

"I know how to get along with humble means, and I also know how to live in prosperity; in any and every circumstance I have learned the secret of being filled and going hungry, **both** of having abundance and suffering need" (Philippians 4:12).

Knowing we all have trouble with this principle of receiving, rather than give to friends in need, many times I was forced to agree to "lend" Christians the money. In their minds (and what allowed them to accept what I wanted to just "give" them), it meant that they were "planning" to pay it back. Again, this was due to them not knowing how to accept freely because they never felt comfortable with receiving.

Years earlier I had learned another Bible principle that we are supposed to just *give*, not **lend** at all (Luke 6:34-38, Deuteronomy 23:19-20) What I love about following the principle of giving rather than lending is because you are instantly set free from the bondage of *expecting* the payment returned to you. Expecting and not receiving what is "owed" is normally the cause of relationships that end bitterly. Am I right? Nevertheless, if someone wants to borrow, we need to lend (Matthew 5:42).

And because I had always given to others with this mindset, to give and not expect that it would be paid back, is why I forgot that anyone owed me anything. This principle was the next lesson I needed to learn and live.

Chapter 17
You Owe Me Nothing

"He seized him and began to choke him, saying,
'Pay back **what** you **owe.'**
—Matthew 18:28

This next lesson I needed to learn and live to move my mountain is found in this parable...

The Parable of the Unmerciful Servant

"Then Peter came to Jesus and asked, "Lord, how many times shall I forgive my brother when he sins against me? Up to seven times?'

"Jesus answered, "I tell you, not seven times, but seventy-seven times.

"Therefore, the kingdom of heaven is like a king who wanted to settle accounts with his servants. As he began the settlement, a man who owed him ten thousand talents was brought to him. Since he was not able to pay, the master ordered that he and his wife and his children and all that he had be sold to repay the debt.

"The servant fell on his knees before him. 'Be patient with me,' he begged, 'and I will pay back everything.' The servant's master took pity on him, canceled the debt and let him go.

"But when that servant went out, he found one of his fellow servants who owed him a hundred denarii [a few dollars]. He grabbed him and began to choke him. 'Pay back what you owe me!' he demanded.

"His fellow servant fell to his knees and begged him, 'Be patient with me, and I will pay you back.'

"But he refused. Instead, he went off and had the man thrown into prison until he could pay the debt. When the other servants saw what had happened, they were greatly distressed and went and told their master everything that had happened.

"Then the master called the servant in. 'You wicked servant,' he said, 'I canceled all that debt of yours because you begged me to. Shouldn't you have had mercy on your fellow servant just as I had on you?' In anger his master turned him over to the jailers to be tortured, until he should pay back all he owed.

"This is how my heavenly Father will treat each of you unless you forgive your brother from your heart."

Most of us have read this parable, and most have also heard a sermon or two on it. Each time we feel uncomfortable and concerned that we may have forgotten someone who needs to be set free from what they believe they "owe" us. At least, that's the way I always react to this story.

Honestly, I am not sure how the Lord brought this principle to my mind, but I do know when, and because I tend to be a person riddled with guilt (not sure if it is due to my Catholic upbringing, my personality, or both), I felt guilty the very *moment* I realized it.

It happened just a few days after my son **paid me back** a considerable sum that I had hoped he would simply "take" as an investment toward his future. Just three days later, after he paid me back and I accepted it is when He reminded me that I needed to be a receiver, not just a giver, that I realized that to be set free from *my* debt, I needed to be certain that I released each and every person who owed me! Unfortunately (and this is why I felt guilty), I assumed that I should have thought of this sooner!

Giving the money back to my son was impossible because my initial response to his handing me the check was to cry and not accept it. But God convicted me (as I shared with you in the last chapter) that many of us are very good "givers", but we also need to be able to *accept* when someone gives *to* us. So, I had accepted his gift, then turned around only three days later to tell his brother that *he* owed me nothing!

[May I say that later, after discussing this with my HH over a cup of coffee, that He showed me this, too, was part of His plan. Of course, it's a journey and He'd led me to take his money while releasing his brother because very soon, my son "Mr. Giver" was about to reap some huge rewards—which he did soon after!]

So, who still owed me? The first person that came to mind was my other son who had borrowed money to pay his taxes. He had worked for my ministry as an independent contractor, while also working part-time somewhere else. As a contractor, it is not the responsibility of the employer to withhold taxes, so when tax time came, he owed a lot, which was bad timing since he was just weeks before his wedding day. So, he ended up borrowing money from me.

Would you believe that it wasn't until the very day that the Lord showed me that I had to release everyone from owing me that I remembered the money I had loaned him? I had totally forgotten his debt, due to the heart of giving the Lord had given me and the principle to give and not lend that He'd taught me in Luke 6:34-38 and Deuteronomy 23:19-20.

Unfortunately, though, at the time there had been some misunderstandings in our relationship and I had taken the "letting go" posture while I trusted God to restore my relationship with him—and, of course, He did, but not until He led me to start a book *Trust GOD to Restore Your Relationships*—a book that's been on my heart for a long time.

Sharing this revelation, telling him that he owed me nothing, was pressing on my heart and rattling my spirit, and it needed to come out somehow. So that morning I called my son and when I finished telling him about what the Lord had revealed to me, as an afterthought I added, "So, if for any reason you think you owe me anything—you don't." His response totally stunned me, when he said, "Are you kidding? I can't believe your timing Mom. For the last three days I have been struggling with how much I owe you, and, knowing your financial situation I just felt I had to do something to begin paying you back. But we just don't have anything to spare [he had just gotten married]."

I was sure he was mistaken about owing me, and I told him so. Nevertheless, I assured him he owed me nothing at all because our Beloved Savior has paid the price for me, so I was officially releasing him! Though my son is not emotional at all, I could hear in his voice that he was deeply touched and wonderfully relieved.

Then, to my surprise, at that exact moment, a floodgate flew open in my brain and I remembered the many times he **had** borrowed from me, never paying me back. But I had forgotten all of them. It was then I realized something else…

You may have released many people from owing you, **but** if you don't tell them they are released, then they are still bound, in prison, even if you unlocked their prison cell long ago! I knew that it meant that the Lord was about to reveal to me others who believed they owed me; the next one was my ex-husband.

Throughout my divorce, and the two years following it, I radically gave my ex everything he asked for, not withholding anything. In addition, I was careful to give him more than he asked for as the principle in Matthew 5:39-42 teaches us. Even so, two and a half years later, just a week after both my sons married, my ex-husband maliciously attacked me and my ministry with a vengeance like none other. I wrote about this, in length, in a previous chapter that, thankfully, the Lord is not going to make me include in this book. The main reason for writing the chapter was to be the "real deal" to my closest friends, family and some RMI ministry team members, in order to have an opportunity to boast about my weaknesses.

Regardless of what he'd done, my ex was on my list to tell him he owed me nothing. Yet, I immediately heard "no" each time this came to my mind. So, I waited and didn't know if I was ever going to release him from what he "owed" me. Long ago are the days that I reason or try to *lean on my own understanding*, no, not due to my newly found wisdom, but primarily due to falling so often! I no longer assume something will happen and try to reason when and why. Instead, I simply wait and trust for an appointed time (Habakkuk 2:2-3).

Without going into details, with this new and malicious attack, to my surprise, rather than turning the other cheek and walking the extra mile that I had come to love, and honestly enjoy, I was led (and wrestled with) "turning over the tables in the temple," not literally, but figuratively. It wasn't until later, then again much later, that I understood the significance of my uncharacteristic actions. Prior to that day, I had, without knowing it, allowed my ex-husband (after our divorce), to continue to run my ministry, thus submitting to him.

Not only was that a problem for me, because I was His bride and no one else's. But it was also wrong to do to women who I was ministering to. By allowing him to tell me what I could and could not do, whether it was post something on my site, print something in a book, or what I could sell and/or give away, I unknowingly had kept him as the head of my ministry. Rats, I was unfaithful once again. I was His bride, but my actions said otherwise. Of course, the moment I asked my precious Husband to forgive me, He had, and I knew He also would give me an opportunity to make it right.

The moment came the afternoon after He'd given me a principle found in Matthew 10:19, "...do not worry about how or what you are to say; for it will be given you in that hour what you are to say." And again, in Luke 12:11, "When they bring you before the synagogues and the rulers and the authorities, do not worry about how or what you are to speak in your defense, or what you are to say." So, no longer "ready" knowing what I would say (1 Peter 3:15) when he called, I simply remained silent. Because I said nothing, not continually agreeing as I always did, he became louder and repeated what he wanted me to do, much more forcefully. Then, finally, at the conclusion of this mini-Armageddon, he stopped and said, what do you want? I calmly replied by saying, "Well, I suppose you owe me an apology." Shock.

Baffled is an understatement. Here I was, releasing everyone and I hear myself saying that he "owes" me an apology? How can I move forward if I am still desperately needing to release two people from owing me?

Do you know that this is also part of God's plan? As I said, it falls under the "wait" principle. Remember how I told you that I knew I needed to *wait* to pay my "back" tithes? Here's one reason why. After waiting to pay the tithe for my second big donation, when the day finally did come, I was elated, and not concerned at all with the cost of the "around the world" ticket that I had to buy—which was more than my tithe should have been. I had, by waiting, renewed my "giving" strength so I could mount up with those lovely eagle wings that allowed me not to faint when it was time to purchase it (Isaiah 40:31).

Then, again, my *wait* to release these two men also served to strengthen me, so that I was ready when the day finally came. Without sharing too much information, let me just say that releasing my ex did happen, appropriately enough, on what would have been my mother's birthday. My children and I had decided a few months earlier that on her birthday, each year (and my father's birthday too, who is also deceased) we would spend that day as a day of remembering and honoring them, doing something special.

So that morning while talking about my mom, I was suddenly reminded of something that my ex-husband had done during the time when my father was dying. It reminded me of him in an entirely different light, turning my heart, I knew then that it was the appointed time for me to email and release him from "owing me" an apology and "anything else" that he might have thought he owed me.

In the Lord's wonderful way, He created the perfect method of pulling down any of his emotional walls when I reminded him of the incident that the Lord had brought to *my* mind. Immediately after I sent it, I did the same thing by writing to both my son and his new wife, letting them know that I released them from the back taxes and anything else they felt they might have owed me.

17. You Owe Me Nothing   153

It took quite a while for me to hear back from each of them, but that simply gave me time to acknowledge that *how* **they responded**, good or bad, was not the point. The point was this—that I was making things right with my Husband, just as withholding freedom from those who owe you doesn't have anything to do with the other person. It is *you* who will be held in bondage, not them, just as the opening parable teaches us.

And now, I believe I am only one step away from releasing *everyone* from the debt they owed me. The last is the most special, it's you—dear bride, you, too, are released!

Whether or not you have been blessed by my ministry, most of us feel "indebted" to giving financially to a particular ministry and often feel as if we "owe" them some sort of tithe or offering. Some women have written that they did, in fact, "owe me" back tithes (some were quite large), yet, as of today, you owe me nothing.

For some of you, you might be feeling my release or pardon came much too late, because you already paid back tithes or your offering. But let me assure you that just as my son was blessed because he paid me back and gave—so will you!

And, if this chapter was not already so long, I would share my testimony of when I was actually told I was released from "owing" on a building pledge, which was my first step in my moving mountain journey. Just let me say that, even though I was told I no longer owed the building pledge, each and every time I ask my Beloved about paying it, He impressed on my heart that this was His plan—that I should pay it. Long story short, two hours after I paid it, I got a check for the entire ten-thousand-dollar pledge!

I am saying this as a warning. Though *I* released you, check with God to be sure this is His plan for you. You may not owe me, but if your Husband wants you to pay back tithes or offerings, or a building pledge or anything else, pay it. Always check with your Husband, and don't listen to what *anyone* tells you if it's contrary to what He told you first. As a powerful reminder, let's finish this chapter by reading the very painful story about the disobedient prophet when he listened to the older prophet instead of what God told him.

"Then he [the older prophet] said to him, 'Come home with me and eat bread.'

"He [the younger prophet] said, 'I cannot return with you, nor go with you, nor will I eat bread or drink water with you in this place.

"For a command came to me by the word of the LORD, 'You shall eat no bread, nor drink water there; do not return by going the way which you came.'

"He [the older prophet] said to him, 'I also am a prophet like you, and an angel spoke to me by the word of the LORD, saying, 'Bring him back with you to your house, that he may eat bread and drink water' But he lied to him.

"So he went back with him, and ate bread in his house and drank water.

"Now it came about, as they were sitting down at the table, that the word of the LORD came to the prophet who had brought him back; and he cried to the man of God who came from Judah, saying, "Thus says the LORD, 'Because you have disobeyed the command of the LORD, and have not observed the commandment which the LORD your God commanded you, but have returned and eaten bread and drunk water in the place of which He said to you, 'Eat no bread and drink no water'; your body shall not come to the grave of your fathers.'

"It came about after he had eaten bread and after he had drunk, that he saddled the donkey for him, for the prophet whom he had brought back.

"Now when he had gone, a lion met him on the way and killed him, and his body was thrown on the road, with the donkey standing beside it; the lion also was standing beside the body. And behold, men passed by and saw the body thrown on the road, and the lion standing beside the body; so they came and told it in the city where the old prophet lived.

"Now when the prophet who brought him back from the way heard it, he said, "It is the man of God, who disobeyed the command of the LORD; therefore the LORD has given him to the lion, which has torn him and killed him, according to the word of the LORD which He spoke to him" (1 Kings 13:15-26).

This startling story teaches us one thing, which is— listen to no one who tells you something that the Lord has not told you. If you are not sure, just ask Him and He will be sure you know His heart when that is what you are searching for (Matthew 7:7).

Now, let me conclude this chapter with this thought and suggestion: Whether we realize it or not, we are holding people in bondage. People we know and love, and maybe even some we despise for what they've done to us or someone else—each is being held captive, and the sad truth is—so are we. How can we hold someone captive when Jesus died to set them and us free from so much?

Set others free, and as you do, you will set yourself free!

Lastly, rather than reading the next chapter of this book, stop right now, close the book, and get alone with your Husband. It'll just take but a moment of your time but will result in a huge reward. Simply ask Him if there is anyone you are holding captive that you need to contact and release. You will be pleasantly surprised, and totally shocked by the results—I sure was.

Chapter 18

By Grace

"For **by grace** you have been saved
Through faith;
And that not of yourselves,
It is the gift of God;
Not as a result of works, so that no one may boast."
—Ephesians 2:8–9

Probably one of the most difficult characteristics of God to understand is His grace. We are so far from this trait as human beings, that by trying to understand it, we destroy its beauty. Preachers are terrified by its meaning and therefore feel the necessity to join it with *works* or the *law* lest they lead their congregation astray.

Grace, in its purest form, means that we are given what we do not deserve based solely on the unimaginable love of God.

God knows our nature and, therefore, is well aware that as adults, when we have lost that innocence and "faith of a child" we have to travel through the journey of works and the law for us to get to the point where we give up and, in our exhaustion or frustration, give it to God— accepting His grace—His unmerited favor.

Even though my mind and my heart embrace His amazing grace, I am no different than anyone else. Surely, I must live within His laws, and as a Christian actually exceed the law as proof of my right standing with God. For some reason we just can't accept that we are in right standing by one thing only—by what our Savior **did**, not what you and I can or will do.

So, in my finances God took me on a little journey (may I say a very difficult journey?) that led me *through* complicated and thorny places to show me things I was ignorant of. One very important to me, to Him, and to our wellbeing is tithing. God set about to teach me the importance of tithing, the dangers of ignoring it, the power of forgiving those who owe me, only to find out that what God is seeking from us, which is not surprising, is not just 10%, but rather 100% of our heart.

God wants His children to be cheerful givers, and this is what the Pharisees missed. Look at these contrasting examples:

"Now this I say, he who sows sparingly will also reap sparingly, and he who sows bountifully will also reap bountifully. Each one must do just as he has purposed in his heart, not grudgingly or under compulsion, for God loves a cheerful giver. And God is able to make all **grace abound** to you, so that always having all sufficiency in everything, you may have an abundance for every good deed" (2 Corinthians 9:6–9). Versus…

"Woe to you, scribes and Pharisees, hypocrites! For you tithe mint and dill and cumin, and have neglected the weightier provisions of the law: justice and mercy and faithfulness; but these are the things you should have done without neglecting the others" (Matthew 23:23).

The Message Bible explains it this way: "You're hopeless, you religion scholars and Pharisees! Frauds! You keep meticulous account books, tithing on every nickel and dime you get, but on the meat of God's Law, things like fairness and compassion and commitment—the absolute basics!—you carelessly take it or leave it. Careful bookkeeping is commendable, but the basics are required. Do you have any idea how silly you look, writing a life story that's wrong from start to finish, nitpicking over commas and semicolons?"

Yes, nitpicking over things that don't matter. Focusing on the outside rather than the inside. Doing all we can to make sure we are in right standing with God so that we have the assurance of being blessed.

Yet, once again, God blesses us *not* because of what we can do, but because of what **He**, our Savior, has done.

It was His death on the cross, with our sins nailed to it, which paid our debt—all of it. What I learned while on my difficult journey was that I no longer needed to be like the Pharisees, counting and figuring dollars and cents; not even doing my best to be sure that I gave above and beyond what I believed He expected of me. The point is— it is all about grace, which is freely given, not earned.

"He has *given freely* to the poor" (Ps. 112:9). For "Blessed are the **poor** in **spirit**, for theirs is the kingdom of heaven" (Matthew 5:3). We were spiritually poor.

"Freely you received, *freely give*" (Matthew 10:8). He freely gave to us; therefore, we need to freely give to others.

"Now we have received, not the spirit of the world, but the Spirit who is from God, so that we may know the things *freely given* to us by God" (1 Corinthians 2:12).

To come to the culmination, the conclusion, the finale, the climax— "He who did not spare His own Son, but delivered Him over for us all, how will He not also with Him *freely give* us all things?" (Romans 8:32).

It took doing everything I could do, and then failing miserably, for me to accept what was mine all along—His grace.

When I realized that I had not officially tithed from my ministry, I saw my sin, and that I had fallen short of what was expected of me— the law of giving 10%. I looked at the huge debt with the realization and the vast inability to pay that debt. That was when the Lord turned my focus on not trying to pay the huge debt (like past sins), but to simply pay the ministry's current tithes as each donation or bookstore earning came in.

Though I will admit that money (banking, figures, and the like) are not my forte or specialty (even though I got straight A's in math when I was in school) this, I was sure, would be a cinch. Wrong. God made sure that I was utterly and helplessly confused, and soon I was unsure if I had paid or if I hadn't paid my tithes on parts of my income, once again, I realized that I needed my Savior.

In an instant, I thoroughly recognized my utter dependence and hopelessness, and that nothing I could do would measure up with a perfect and holy God—which is just the point! Nothing you or I could do will pay our debt: not for our sins, nor with tithing, which are both based on the law requiring works "because by the **works** of the Law no **flesh** will be justified in His sight; for *through* the Law comes the knowledge of sin" (Romans 3:20)… "nevertheless knowing that a man is not justified by the **works** of the Law but through faith in Christ Jesus, even we have believed in Christ Jesus, so that we may be justified by faith in Christ and not by the **works** of the Law; since by the **works** of the Law *no* **flesh** will be justified" (Galatians 2:16).

The law was given to prove the impossibility of men being right in the sight of God, which proved their need for a Savior. It was the Pharisees who tried to prove that they did everything right: from tithing, fasting, and even knowing the scriptures (which foretold the coming of Jesus, but they missed it entirely), were worthless because all of these are issues of the heart.

God took me on a journey of grace, but to find my way there, I had to fail miserably while trying to keep the law. I couldn't keep it, and neither can you.

Yet you might be saying, "Michele, are you kidding? I have been faithful to tithe and do it easily! You may not be able to figure out 10% and give it to your storehouse, but I certainly can." But you have missed the point…

Once our Savior came and left us His Spirit, we were no longer under the law, meaning we were no longer expected to abide by it. But, as Paul told us, it does not mean that we should go out and break the law either. However, if we try to abide by the law, and fail in just one point, we are guilty of all. So, our choice is to both follow the law and try to live by it or—choose grace—I am choosing grace!

Once a believer experiences His grace, which is freely given to us by God through His Son, then we become like Him and want to also give freely. We forgive freely because He has forgiven us freely, for those who do not forgive freely are not forgiven...isn't that what it says?

"For if you forgive others for their transgressions, your heavenly Father will also forgive you. But if you do not forgive others, then your Father will not forgive your transgressions" (Matthew 6:14–15).

"Whenever you stand praying, forgive, if you have anything against anyone, so that your Father who is in heaven will also forgive you your transgressions. But if you do not forgive, neither will your Father who is in heaven forgive your transgressions" (Mark 11:25–26).

And after the man refused to forgive the man who owed him, which caused him to then be turned over to the "torturers until he should repay all that was owed him." Jesus said, "My heavenly Father will also do the same to you, if each of you does not forgive his brother *from your **heart**"* (Matthew 18:35).

It's always a heart issue with God. Ezekiel prophetically spoke of what would happen after Jesus came and sent us His spirit:

"And I will give them one heart, and put a new spirit within them and I will take the heart of stone out of their flesh and give them a heart of flesh" (Ezekiel 11:19).

"Moreover, I will give you a new heart and put a new spirit within you; and I will remove the heart of stone from your flesh and give you a heart of flesh" (Ezekiel 36:26).

And a heart issue, now I know, goes for tithing and giving too. What my Heavenly Husband explained to me at the end of my journey is that His grace is sufficient and that long ago He put a spirit of giving in my heart—He put Himself. He began to reveal to me, almost supernaturally, how His Spirit had actually caused me to always give **more** than a 10% tithing would, one by one.

Time after time, from the moment I was given my ministry back and I was in charge of its finances, my darling Husband showed me that I'd given each time He had instructed me to. I did exactly what my ex-husband was afraid I'd do—I began giving everything I had away. Our books were sent out free to those who couldn't afford them, and I "foolishly" reduced the price of our books to our members so they simply paid our cost (meaning we would make nothing). I no longer charged to be a member or required that they purchase books to be a member, and I gave abundantly to missions and to anywhere else I could find—just because I felt so free to simply give!

Once I saw what He had done, in a moment of relief, my eyes filled with tears of gratitude—grateful for a Savior whose grace was more than sufficient.

The Lord showed me that not only had I given, I had given freely, cheerfully, and amazingly much more than a meager 10%, as with a religious tither would do. The records were all there but were hidden from me until I had reached the end of my journey so that I would experience firsthand, once again, about His amazing grace.

His grace is the substance that cannot be mixed or joined with the law or our works, for in doing so, it becomes ineffective. With tithing, as it is with so many areas of our lives, we try to follow the law, stumble in just one point, making us guilty of all, as we drowned in a sea of condemnation. "For whoever keeps the whole law and yet stumbles in one point, he has become guilty of all" (James 2:10).

Praise God "Therefore there is now *no condemnation* for those who are in Christ Jesus" (Romans 8:1).

This is Good News to the Believer who is having a love affair with their Beloved, but troublesome to those who are followers of religion.

For you, dear bride, there is no longer any need to count, worry, or wonder if you are measuring up **when** you are walking in the joy of the Lord and in His love—by His grace. Relieved? I am.

Chapter 19
Valley of Humiliation

"Yea, though I walk through
the valley of the shadow of death,
I will fear no evil: for Thou art with me"
—Psalm 23:4

When I began this journey on the road to being debt free, I conveniently forgot a portion of all my previous journeys when the Lord has asked me to walk with Him *through*—the Valley of Humiliation. I have been down this humble road before, many times. Some have been deeper and darker than others, but I know now that I never really know how deep it's going to be, not even when I have turned the corner to see that God, once again, is calling me down into a dark hole.

"The LORD … raises up all who are **bowed down**" (Psalm 145:14).

It is human to fear this dreaded valley, and often we do, so that as a result of our fear we find we add to our fear **guilt** since everyone knows that as a "Christian" we shouldn't fear, right? Yet, God knows our frailties and that is why He doesn't send us down through the valley alone, instead, He promises to send Someone very special to come with us.

"Look! I see four men loosed and walking about in the midst of the fire without harm, and the appearance of the **fourth** is like a Son of the gods!" Daniel 3:25 "Even though I walk through the valley of the shadow of death, I fear no evil, for *You are with me;* Your rod and Your staff, they comfort me" (Psalm 23:4). Having our Heavenly Husband walking with us is *the main reason He leads us down.* He

19. Valley of Humiliation

wants us to know that *what* we naturally fear is something we really don't *need* to fear.

Time and again we prove that we are simply children, His child bride, and not so grown up after all. So, God, like many fathers, will walk us through the dark places in life to show us that everything is really alright. And depending on the sort of relationship we have with our Father will determine how we are able to sleep at night while traveling into these dark places. Am I right?

During my first real walk *through* that well known "valley" that so many of us dread, I was really just getting to know the Lord on a deeply intimate level as my Husband. He was my Savior, sure, but this is when He became my Lord. It happened during the period of my life when I was young and had just been abandoned by my husband, alone with four small children, and no future in sight. That's when He chose me to take a little walk with Him. Unfortunately, for almost two years I didn't sleep well at all. Many of you are there right now, aren't you?

Darling, if that is you, please don't beat yourself up about it. God is only saying that to rid yourself of that fear and those sleepless nights, you simply need to get closer to Him, to the point that you feel safe. So, simply snuggle up, listen to Him, and soon you will feel that safety that is yours because He loves you, because you are His, which is nothing you have to earn. If you are not sure just how to go about "cuddling up" with Him, tell your Husband or your Father that too, and He will accomplish it without you having to figure it out. I know.

Now back to that valley. It was many years after my first valley experience, when all of a sudden, I turned a corner and found myself facing the downward slope again. This valley of humiliation was very similar to the one I was all too familiar with, but this time there was much more at stake. However, during those years, I had gained a real intimacy that radically changed the way I walked that walk with my Husband—we were now Lovers. If you want to learn more, the best way is to read *Finding the Abundant Life* (by losing it, based on Matthew 16:25), and then *Living the Abundant Life*. Both are available for free on one of RMI's websites: RestoreMinistries.net.

Another Valley?

It was only two years later that my ministry and life took a surprising turn when, out of nowhere, my website suddenly got shut down—alas, another "new" valley was waiting for me to discover. When I realized what was ahead, I can't say I began to fear, but I will say that, unfortunately, I did begin to dread. And that dread is a lot like fretting, and fretting, Psalm 37 says, leads to all kinds of things that I didn't want to get myself caught in.

About the same time, I noticed something else even more alarming: the real "in love" feeling with my Husband that I had experienced during and after my divorce that lasted for nearly two glorious years, was really not there! Oh, of course, I loved my Husband dearly and could feel He loved me too. But that "in love" feeling that I thought would last *for all eternity* had begun to fade as it does with most married couples: the awe and wonder began to be less intense. I knew it was all due to the stress and busyness of my day-to-day living, and no doubt due to the trials that now plagued my life.

I cannot tell you how desperately I wanted to be "in love" again; I wanted that feeling and intimacy back. So, as I always say you should do, I simply asked my Husband, just like the first time. "Darling, how can I get closer to You? How can I feel that 'in love' emotion we women love to drench ourselves in?" Funny thing is, I guess God's solution happened just two days later when I took a turn along my journey that headed down through this new valley.

Who of us doesn't realize that our intimacy (how close we feel to our Husband) is due to the valleys in our lives? And, the deeper the valley, the deeper the intimacy we get to experience. Our heads know it, but our hearts often faint within us when we are asked to take a similar journey since there is naturally a fear of the unknown.

Of course, God is faithful—you and I both know that. So, He chose to start my journey by sending me someone else who needed encouragement. Why? Because there is no better way to get encouraged than to encourage someone else. Did you know that? And that's why so many people are running around *without courage*—they fail to embrace this principle and many other principles written in the Bible as solutions to their problems.

The main principle, once you really know your Bible, is this: "*Everything* in the kingdom of God is the **opposite** of the world." We might know it, but we don't live it. So, when we need money, we hoard it instead of giving it away. When we are hurt, we hurt back rather than bless our enemies. And when we need encouragement, we get all wrapped up in ourselves not realizing that our encouragement comes in the form of encouraging someone else. So, when someone needs something and is sent by God to "come'a knocking at our door," we pretend we are not at home! You understand I am saying this figuratively, but it could even be applied literally.

The same principle that "in the kingdom of God *everything* is the **opposite** of the world" goes for when we are given a promise that we know is from God, that He is calling us to do something really *awesome* for Him. And this thing He is calling us to do will "eventually" promote us, and possibly put us in the limelight—but first, God faithfully calls us to ***descend*** into greatness. For far too many Believers, this descent, without their understanding of this foundational principle, convinces them that this **can't** be *from* God; therefore, they *refuse* to "lower themselves," or "stoop so low" missing the point that the journey begins with descent.

Even though we are Christians, which means followers of Christ who **should** *appear* peculiar, and in particular, humble, we use all the same excuses and lingo (such as self-esteem or self-respect, etc.) as every other human on the planet would use to refuse the descent, all because we haven't learned the fundamental principle that "in the kingdom of God everything is the opposite of the world." Are you getting it? Good, now we let's move on.

Dear bride, since *you* are reading this book, I have to assume that you are more like me: You *know* this principle, but it's so easy to forget when it comes around again; isn't it? Just remember, your Husband loves you along with *all* of your frailties, every single one of them. He is only trying to rid you of anything and everything that stands in the way of the sort of happiness only a bride has: the joy that is unspeakable, so full you could burst. And the way to rid yourself of the fear that is surely trying to take hold of you is to draw ever closer to your Husband, and to also use what He said He'd send us—*testimonies* to overcome what your mind and what other people want to tell you.

"And they overcame him [the wicked one] because of the blood of the Lamb and because of the **word** *of their* **testimony**, and they did not love their life even when faced with death" (Revelation 12:11).

Most of the time God uses my own testimonies to encourage me. He reminds me of things He has already done for me, and that's just what He did this time. This time He told me that the freedom that I experienced after going *through* my divorce was what it would be like when I was done going *through* this financial valley. Before being divorced again, there were many things I couldn't do like I can do now. It is an entire life full of freedoms—just one was to be free to fly around the world several times! When I was married, my husband (at the time), wouldn't even allow me to go to New York for my fiftieth birthday even though he asked what I really wanted to do.

Yet, less than a year later, I was walking freely on the streets of New York, *and* walking all over Africa, Europe, Asia, and South America! Reminding me of my own testimony made it easy to see what was up ahead, **but** I also needed to remember that the freedom I have now took me descending into the valley of humiliation when my restored marriage fell apart. When my husband once again fell into the pit of adultery, I was asked for another divorce that I had to go through, but that's what brought me undue freedom and blessings into my life, as well as new testimonies to encourage others and to ultimately encourage me.

Can I break away to say something that will help you remember how important it is for you to share each of your testimonies: big and small? I think of our own personal testimonies in the same way that people today are able to give blood or bone marrow to themselves so it's ready for when they need it later. Many parents save their babies' cord blood in blood banks for future needs. There are so many of my own testimonies, some large and others small, which have kept me going through the worst or hardest of times! And each one of my testimonies was shared and was designed to encourage others—so give life by allowing and sharing testimonies—because they will someday return to overflow and encourage you! "Give, and it will be given to you. They will pour into your lap a good measure—pressed down, shaken together, and running over. For by your standard of measure it will be measured to you in return" (Luke 6:38).

It was when my neighbor came to tell me that she was losing her home that my testimonies came in handy. In our neighborhood, it has become an epidemic, as it has all over our nation. The thought has crossed my mind, I must admit, especially since my ministry had basically shut down and I currently have no real income. I mean, why not me? And yet, each time I spoke to my Husband about it, He'd ask me, "Michele, do you really think you are going to lose your house?"

Why is it that the Lord loves to answer a question with a question?

My answer has always sort of been, "Well, yes and no, or should I say no and yes? No, I don't believe that I will" I say that in faith. And yet, I didn't think that the *freedom* to be His bride, which I enjoy now, would have come from going *through* divorce again; therefore, maybe it does mean that I will have to go through losing my house, and everything in it, to find financial freedom. Honestly, it takes someone a lot wiser than I am to know what is up ahead, and just how deep the valley that I am heading down really is.

Yet, no matter how deep it goes, one thing is certain—on the other side it will be everything my Husband promised to me, **and** even more importantly, I **get** to walk through it close to my Beloved Husband, which makes the journey ever so sweet. And when I have doubts, all I need to look at is the very recent testimony of another bride, the missionary I spoke about in previous chapters, who submitted her praise report. Her valley was so deep, so dark, so full of mocking, jeering, rejection, and every other horrible thing, some unimaginable, but it was down in this valley that led her to the mountaintop—singing the sweetest of praises.

When this bride was just a young teen, she went to see a woman who had escaped (barely alive) from an eastern country in Africa. After hearing her incredible and moving testimony she went up to meet her, when in the middle of our talking her companion from Africa got down on her knees in front of her, laid her hands on her feet and said, "These feet will walk on African soil bringing hope." From that day, she said she felt called to go to Africa. But the road to get there was meant to prepare her for what she would face when she arrived.

This summer, she said, seemed so close to fulfilling her dreams, everything was in place, all doors were opened, then suddenly one door, where she was to reside while in Africa, slammed shut. Week after week she waited and wondered if she would ever go. It was during this waiting period that she learned firsthand some of what our Savior experienced in betrayal. In addition, she had two near-death experiences, which made many of her closest friends tell her that what she was trying to do was too dangerous, that the enemy was after her, and to reconsider.

Yet, GOD, YET **GOD**, in His lovingkindness, His very nature, had a love story that had been written just for her from the beginning of time, that you will read in the next chapter, "My Johnathan."

"Thank you my precious Lord, Savior, and my Beloved for blessing me with my own valley and the courage to trust You as I do. I love You more every moment of every day!"

Chapter 20

My Jonathan

"Eye hath not seen,
Nor ear heard,
Neither have entered into the heart of man,
The things which God hath prepared for them
That love Him."
—1 Corinthians 2:9 KJV

It's been just a few days since we arrived home from an amazing and a completely unexpected trip to Orlando, Florida. Every morning as I looked out over our view from our resort, just days before Christmas, while sipping freshly squeezed orange juice, I asked the Lord, "Why?" Why did He bring us there? His answer was life-changing, and His answer is for you my dear—it was our Jonathan.

Well, just who, you ask, is Jonathan? In the last chapter I promised to share a love story with you that emerged during the valley of humiliation our first missionary was asked to go through. As I began to tell you, it happened so suddenly when light began to shine in her dark, terrifying tunnel.

In the midst of her pain, there was a young man from South Africa who was looking for a bloke (guy friend) to correspond with while he was living in London and suddenly stumbled on her social media page saying she was going to be a missionary to Africa to work in an orphanage, so he reached out to see if he could help find somewhere to live when he realized it was a she. Jonathan wrote again recommending a "fantastic church" that he said she should attend when she arrived. When she saw the name of the church, she was amazed to see that it was the very same church where I did a radio program while ministering in South Africa, and where her hostess worked—this "coincidence" got her attention.

The young man began praying for her via email and on her social media page. Very soon these two young people began praying 2 to 3 hours each and every day!!! I found out from her mother that her daughter would miss dinner because no one could find her; later, she realized that her daughter was on the floor of her closet PRAYING with this young man rather than eating.

When she would get off the phone, her mom would ask what they were talking about. Rather than the normal things a young couple would talk about, she said, their conversations were always centered on spiritual issues. It seemed as if every day she would tell her that he had said something "radical," then said, "Wow, that's what Michele always says in her ministry!"

On one occasion, I heard that they had been chatting for about 30 minutes when he cut in on her to tell her that they had spoken all that time, but it was **not** centered around God!! He told her that their relationship *had* to be based on **Him** or it was a worthless relationship. Clearly that was when our sweet missionary was convinced that this young man was for her, her parents were also convinced (and I was convinced too when I heard)!

Once their relationship was solid, the Lord opened the doors for her to go to Africa just as easily as He had closed them. And when He did open the doors, He let in a beam of light into this young missionary's life. Where there was once pain, there was joy; where there was once ridicule, there was praise. Where there was once abandonment, there was acceptance. God blessed her with Jonathan.

Though she was told that as a foreign volunteer she would not be caring for the orphans herself, but work in the office, our missionary spent many hours holding, caring and loving these helpless, hurting babies. Though the door had been shut to her residing with the hostess she originally had, a new dear friend of mine opened her home when God turned the heart of her husband and she was able to stay in the very same room where I had been; the very room where my friend and I had first spoken of sending a missionary to Africa!

Then something so wonderful and precious happened, something so dear to my heart—Jonathan's mother and father insisted that she spend her weekends with them—opening their home and hearts to her. As with so many of us, I'd written in other books how we mothers want our children to have what we did not have because one relationship that caused me much pain was the rejection of my in-laws when I was married. Though the Lord healed that hurt (after, that is, I finally took it to **Him** rather than expecting my husband at the time to mend it, which I wrote in one of my books), I love to see young couples have in-laws who love and cherish their children's spouses as their own.

God has graciously blessed my own married children with just that—in-laws who love and treat them as their own children! So, for this sweet missionary, her soon-to-be in laws purchased a ticket for her to travel with them to London to spend the holidays with Jonathan and meet him face-to-face for the first time. This is just a picture of what is ahead for many of you when you believe for amazing things!

Watching what God did for this sweet missionary, and what He asked her to go through to obtain her miracle has served to encourage me so many times, and so many others who had a front seat to her valley of humiliation followed by a mountaintop experience. The first one was my youngest daughter.

The beginning of her Jonathan experience was when she came to me asking for her Christmas money. After her dad left, I found it such a blessing to let my children choose what they wanted for their gifts, so I began giving each of them a sum of money to buy and wrap their own gifts. But this year there was **no** money for Christmas. After avoiding her questions, I finally had to tell her that this year there *may* not be any gifts under the tree. Being so young and seeing how God always provided, it isn't surprising that a day later I found her with tears in her eyes at the thought of no gifts for Christmas. Not knowing really how to help her, I heard her say, "Don't worry mommy, each time I hear Christmas songs, or see holiday decorations, I simply say, "I trust You Father."

News of her Jonathan came on a week before Christmas. It had been such a horrible morning when it *suddenly* changed as my son, the one who always tithes and gives his money as the Lord leads him, handed me an envelope filled with the usual amount for each of the children. But that's not all, only **ten minutes** later I got a call from my dearest neighbor that they were sending us on an all-expense paid trip to Orlando, Florida for a week!

In just 72 hours, God orchestrated each and every last detail, including a rental car and someone to pay for it! Then my other daughter's Jonathan came shortly afterwards: actually, the day before we left to come home. My other daughter was telling me a few months earlier how she desperately wanted a friend. She discussed the possibilities of a suitable friend when I broke in. I said, "Darling, you could look high and low for someone suitable, but friends, good friends, are hard to find. Why not give it to the Lord? Then you know it is His choice for you." She did.

The day before we left Florida, I got a surprise email from my niece. She visited our family for the first time two years prior and during her visit she was wonderfully saved and baptized, sharing her testimony with thousands about being raised in a Hindu home. So, another "Jonathan" is coming in just a few months, and now she has something to really look forward to. Not just a friend, but her closest cousin, who is like a sister to her!

May I also tell you about my neighbor's Jonathan? Faced with the possibility of losing her home, God had a plan that far exceeded her valley of humiliation—a new home! In the "Twelfth hour" a prophesy was spoken of on television when her husband jumped up and said it was for them! While still standing, the phone rang; it was the man who owned the house that they had wanted to buy, but that he would not sell three years earlier!

Do I need to tell you what happened? Yes, the home that they had desired years earlier is now where they are living!! It is twice as large with acreage, not just a yard! Are you feeling encouraged yet? If not, I have just one more story. It centers around two precious ladies I had the pleasure of meeting while I was in Orlando.

20. My Jonathan

For several years, two dear friends (who worked together) had gone through my first Abundant Life books, then one of them said, "I am gonna find this lady, Michele." God did more than allow her to find me—He had **me** find *her!* When I realized we were headed for Florida, I contacted my dear friend who lived in Florida and asked her to contact any bride living near Orlando. I'm convinced that God sent me to Florida for these two brides, just to let them know that He loved them as His own.

The Lord led me to share many things the evening we met. Yet there was one point that each kept bringing me back to, asking me to tell it to them again. "What was that you said, about waiting for…?" "Oh, waiting for my Jonathan you mean? Yes, right now I am waiting for my Jonathan—but you do understand I am not waiting for a man, right?" They giggled.

My Jonathan, and your Jonathan dear reader (and what I told these two brides in Orlando), is that blessing that will fulfill the deepest desires of your heart. It is sure to come upon you *suddenly*. It will be revealed to you in the darkest hour of your life, when you least expect it, and all because you sought Him, trusted Him, and loved Him above all else.

"But as it is written, 'Eye hath not seen, nor ear heard, neither have entered into the heart of man, the things which God hath prepared for them that love Him'" (1 Corinthians 2:9 KJV).

My neighbor's Jonathan experience was different than mine, and both my daughters' Jonathan experiences were different than yours will be. The two Orlando brides, though close friends, each have their own Jonathan experiences that were hidden deep in their hearts. My Jonathan experience continues to change as the years go by. For instance, my Jonathan experience was much different each time my husband left me. The first time God gave me my Jonathan experience when my marriage was restored. Then, several years later, He gave me my Jonathan experience by allowing me to belong only to my Husband, my Beloved, rather than restoring my marriage.

This time, my Jonathan experience will be what I need: financial freedom, similar, as the Lord has told me, to the freedom I gained when He became my Husband.

Whatever it is that is hidden deep in your heart, dear bride, the Lord has taken notice of it and is working the details out right now. Though the days seem long and might even be closing in on your "twelfth hour" as it was for my neighbor and her family—trust me, it will come! All you need to do is to snuggle into the arms of your Husband so that you can feel His presence, His love, and His strength.

While there, you will find that all else, all your problems, your questions, your doubts and your fears, will melt away. All that will be left is you, your Husband, and joy unspeakable as you are filled with His love pouring over all those who are closest to you!

"Give, and it will be given to you. They will pour into your lap a good measure—pressed down, shaken together, and running over. For by your standard of measure it will be measured to you in return" (Luke 6:38).

Chapter 21

Mountain Moved

"You will say to this mountain,
'Move from here to there,' and it will move;
And nothing will be impossible to you."
—Matthew 17:20

It was actually several chapters ago, and even more alarming, six months ago that I actually wrote the majority of this chapter. It was chapter 12 then, when I first began writing "Mountain Moved." To prove that I still have "the faith of a child" even though I am now in my fifties, after chapter 11 was posted on the RMI site and my mountain hadn't moved (my debt had ***not*** been thrown into the depths of the sea), I posted **a** (note this is singular) testimony from a ministry member who watched God do the impossible, and her mountain of debt was thrown into the sea. She wrote to tell me her father had sold some property and gave her cash to buy her home— her marital home that the courts said had to be sold so the money could be split with her ex. Instead of selling, she bought her husband out and now completely owns her home!

The next week, when my mountain again hadn't moved (but now I was so sure than ever it would!) I posted a second testimony from a member who told of a similar story. Her home had gone into foreclosure and in the "twelve-hour" someone had come to pay off their home entirely! My faith was soaring. Then, with a sigh, the third week found me gathering even more testimonies that had come into RMI, and as I posted each, I was still believing God for my Jonathan and my mountain moved. Yet, even in the midst of all the evidence that He'd do the same for me, I began to really wonder if He would do this for me.

Why share all this with you? Why not keep it to myself?

Well, most people, I imagine, would keep it to themselves or pretend to never doubt. But I found out just recently that I am *known* for being completely "transparent." Transparent is a lot like letting people see you underdressed or without your makeup on or letting your hair down—I think you get the point. But more importantly, I believe that you need to know, and I need to remember, that things just don't happen as quickly as we want them to or hope they will.

Looking at the facts, and facing my situation honestly, I basically believed things just couldn't get any worse; therefore, they had to get better: meaning, the mountain would soon, very soon, move or fall!

I was wrong.

If that is not bad enough, I, only a few days ago, was going to change the name of this chapter to "Mountain Crumbling!" Though it hadn't fallen in one mighty swoop, it was crumbling slowly but surely.

The first boulder that fell was when a credit card company contacted *me* and offered, I didn't even have to ask, to lower the percentage rate, and not only that—they backed this rate up to when I had opened the account, which saved me thousands of dollars!! This all occurred due to my not being able to pay the minimum amount, which I had prayed in earnest about (as to what I should do). Is this encouraging or what?

The second boulder that fell was even more incredible! Another credit card payment I could not pay, but this one led me down, down, down through a familiar valley of humiliation. The credit card company told me they could not "work with me" because I was not the "primary" cardholder; my ex-husband was. It took two days of speaking to the Lord about this, to be absolutely sure I understood what He was actually asking me to do, before I moved forward and did it.

In a moment of sheer humility, which felt like total humiliation, I had to write an email explaining the situation to both he and his wife. Why? Because though he had ruined my credit when he divorced me, with an extra lawsuit crippling me financially, I knew that not letting him know I couldn't make the payment had the potential of hurting *his* credit. Do I need to remind you of what Jesus said? "You have heard that it was said, 'an eye for an eye, and a tooth for a tooth' But I say to you, do not resist an evil person; but whoever slaps you on your right cheek, turn the other to him also" (Matthew 5:38–39). So, I got close enough to get slapped and boy was it a doozy.

As I began to compose the email I could hear the "I told you so" because my ex-husband assured me when he left me that my crazy, overzealous ways would someday result in my losing everything. But now looking at this verse in Matthew, I see that I *needed* to be willing to put myself in a place to get slapped again (in the figurative sense).

To make it even more difficult to do the right thing, do you remember when you read about my daughter's Johnathan in the last chapter? Would you believe that this occurred at the very same time I needed to send this email? In other words, here I was writing to tell my ex-husband I couldn't "afford" to pay a credit card bill, yet I was about to take a weeklong Florida vacation!!

Okay, sure, I felt I needed to explain. I even went so far as to write a P.S. fully explaining that the trip was given to us, all expenses paid, blah, blah, blah—that I later removed. Why? It only took reflecting on it a moment to hear what I had told my daughter just weeks earlier, "The people who want to believe the worst in you, will. The people who want to think the best of you, will. Therefore, you need to rid yourself of worrying what other people think and just focus on your relationship with the Lord, which makes you know you are in right standing with God, your Father."

I suppose it goes without saying that sending an email like this, right before my "vacation" had the potential of ruining our trip while I was waiting for the reply. However, after a day of thinking about it, I finally was able to fully surrender it to my Husband. Is He faithful? You bet!! I didn't get my reply until the day after we returned home. And to my utter surprise, shock is more the word, I got a short email that I had to read several times before it seemed real: "We are taking care of the credit card situation so that burden is lifted from you. Have a wonderful Christmas with the children."

Now can you see why I planned to rename this chapter "Mountain Crumbling"? Though I still had plenty of debt, it appeared that God had begun to turn the tide and my mountain was indeed crumbling and would soon fall completely. That was then, but oh so suddenly the enemy reared his ugly head! My ex-husband? Oh, no my dear, "For our struggle is not against flesh and blood, but against the rulers, against the powers, against the world forces of this darkness, against the spiritual forces of wickedness in the heavenly places" (Ephesians 6:12).

Almost a month after my Merry Christmas email, I received a follow up email that made my heart faint within me. It stated that I had been turned over to the fraud department, they were advised to report the card as stolen, was told that I had misled them, and so on and so forth. And for two days I fought trembling when that boulder, which was falling, hit me—*months* of payments were charged back to the merchants and they wanted their money, all of it, now! The credit card company sent me a copy of the handwritten letter my husband sent them, explaining the card had been stolen from his wallet, and he wanted an arrest warrant issued. The police were coming to arrest me, so I had to tell my son so he knew what to do, because I was concerned the minor children would be taken into custody.

What of the other boulder that I thought fell? When the next statement came it did not have a reduced amount, nor did it state that I had received a reduced percentage rate. As a matter of fact, the rate had increased by 4%...

When we hear the testimonies of faithful men and women who God has used to bring about the miracles that give us our spiritual strength and the courage to face our own mountains, I believe we often forget that these were *real* people who really were experiencing the *very real* possibility that their mountain may not fall—their miracle or deliverance may just not happen. And, in response to walking out their beliefs, things actually got terribly worse.

21. Mountain Moved

We see it with those awesome young Hebrew boys. Note their words while standing before the king about to meet their death, or deliverance, but experiencing something far greater. "Shadrach, Meshach and Abed-nego replied to the king, 'O Nebuchadnezzar, we do not need to give you an answer concerning this matter. If it be so, our God whom we serve is able to deliver us from the furnace of blazing fire; and He will deliver us out of your hand, O king. **But even if He does not,** let it be known to you, O king, that we are not going to serve your gods or worship the golden image that you have set up'" (Daniel 3:16–18).

Are we so foolish or ignorant to think that our Bible heroes, or today's heroes of faith, do not experience the same questions, doubts, and emotions that you and I feel when facing a mountain? When we are put in a place of defeat, destruction, or even embarrassment as we stand before our mountain, or before our furnace, we *know* that the God we serve is *able* to deliver us, but will He? Like the young boys, what matters is that we stay true to our beliefs no matter what God chooses to do or not do for us.

As I finish this book, I am still not sure which it will be for me. I had no idea if I would write the testimony of my mountain of debt falling into the sea, or if I would instead post this chapter on my site, ending with still "hoping against hope" (Romans 4:18) from the cell of the local jail. But last night I came to an amazing revelation that took me by surprise. This thought had me blubbering like a baby, and even now I am having trouble containing my tears enough to try and get my thoughts and feelings down on paper.

Over the past few days, this weekend specifically, I was at a wedding where I spoke to so many people with whom I hadn't seen or spoken to for several years. As we got reacquainted and I shared just where I had been and why they hadn't seen me, they inevitably asked if my husband (saying his name) traveled with me. This led me to tell them what had happened (my husband divorcing me and marrying the woman he was involved with and the financial crisis I was facing), and it took them by surprise—actually shock was more their response.

However, each time I was able to share with them just a few highlights of what the Lord had done *for* me: the person who I now am, and the blessing of being His bride (wanting no other), when they asked if I had married again (seeing the ring I wear as a sign that I am "taken" and not available).

All this reminiscing really stayed in my mind, and then just last night, I realized that the "love affair" that I had been experiencing with the Lord was the thing that I was most grateful for. Yet, the second just as precious, was what I discovered and what made me weep last night. Due to the divorce, I was put in a place of being able to *choose* to walk in unknown danger and peril.

For the first time since I had lived with my parents, I no longer had anyone stand in the way of me doing the most radical, most zealous, most foolish things I have been *allowed* to do. And the gratitude was all due to the years of being married, feeling imprisoned, because I *longed* to take God at His Word to the point that I would have everything to lose if He didn't show up.

As a child, or if you are married, you do not have this privilege. There is protection set in place that prevents you from radical feats, and I am sure, due to the hard fact that you and I are not (or were not) yet ready, and those radical feats would probably have turned out badly.

Yet, in the state I am in now, taking the Lord's truth and running with it means that I can put myself in the place that I have no idea how this (or anything else) is going to turn out —no earthly idea at all! It all could end badly, but as I said to the Lord last night ***"I am just so terribly grateful that I had the opportunity to be just one crazy person in this world that is willing, and excited, to go out on a limb, hopefully for You, knowing it might not hold the weight of what I believe."***

There is no way I can be so lofty to think that I know for sure how it ends or that I am on the right track. Yes, when I speak from faith there is no doubt—none at all. No one but God really knows how anything will turn out, do they?

For all the hoopla, I for one am, and forever will be, grateful for this chance. Oh, my, there I go again with the tears.

Of course, it would have been easier for me to write this with a testimony done, complete, while standing, in victory, on top of my fallen mountain shouting Hallelujah. However, I just wanted you to know, and have the opportunity to profess how I really feel on this side of my mountain moving.

Whether my mountain moves or not, I will post this chapter and print this book. If it doesn't work, it has, and had, nothing to do with the Lord's faithfulness; it had everything to do with my own.

For you, dear bride, let me assure you that no matter who is pursuing you unjustly, who or what is standing in the way of what you know God has promised you, or how horrible the circumstances in your life are right now, God is more than able to change everything in an instant! Why is your answer veiled? Why do you still wait? Why are things continually getting worse instead of better?

Simply think back to previous times and what God did for you (and for others) to hear God say to you…

"'For I **know** the **plans** that I have for you,' declares the LORD, '**plans** for welfare and not for calamity to give you a future and a hope'" (Jeremiah 29:11).

Therefore, "For the vision is yet for the appointed time; it hastens toward the goal and it will not fail though it **tarries**, **wait** for it; for it will certainly come, it will not delay" (Habakkuk 2:3).

And certainly, you and "I would have **despaired** unless I had believed that I would see the goodness of the LORD in the land of the **living**" (Psalm 27:13).

And no matter what may be coming at you, remember "When the disciples saw Him walking on the sea, they were terrified, and said, 'It is a ghost!' And they cried out in fear. But immediately Jesus spoke to them, saying, 'Take courage, it is I; do not be afraid.' Peter said to Him, 'Lord, if it is You, command me to come to You on the water'" (Matthew 14:26–28). So, get out and walk toward Him. Never forgetting this final promise...

"These things I have spoken to you, so that in Me you may have peace. In the world you have tribulation, but take courage; I have overcome the world" (John 16:33).

Epilog

"And there are also many other things…
which if they were written in detail,
I suppose that even the world itself would not contain
the books which were written."
—John 21:25

It's been exactly 10 years since this book was first published, and that version didn't include this Epilog.

First, praise God, I never spent any time in jail. The credit card company graciously dropped the charges, after they transferred the credit card debt into my name in order for me to pay it off.

Secondly, my mountain finally fell, not just crumbled, and was cast into the sea.

As I predicted, it did not fall as I'd ever imagined it would. After I had the opportunity of giving my house back to the mortgage company, something so unheard of at the time (yet a year later everyone was walking away from their homes,) I received a surprising phone call from one of my dearest friends who lives overseas. She asked me where I was going to go, after hearing I'd given my house back and I said, "I have no idea." She got very excited and shouted, "You're coming to live here! I wondered why I couldn't find a one-bedroom and why God had given me two—it was for you!!!" To confirm this was His plan, He led me to find a flight that was so cheap my friend couldn't believe I was serious. So, a few weeks later I packed just 3 suitcases, gave everything I owned away to family, and I flew to my new brand-new home that had a view of Lake Geneva in Switzerland!

This all happened after my deepest valley of all time. My husband took our children for a visit, then refused to return them. Very soon, after some unimaginable stunts to stop me from trying to get the children back, it was clear that for **me** to remain in this country wasn't at all safe for me or for my children. "Then Jesus said to His disciples, 'If anyone wishes to come after Me, let him deny himself, and take up his cross, and follow Me. For whoever wishes to save his life shall lose it; but whoever loses his life for My sake shall find it'" (Matthew 16:24-25). "Agree with thine adversary quickly, while thou art in the way with him" (Matthew 5:25 KJV). "Keeping away from strife is an honor for a man, but any fool will quarrel" (Proverbs 20:3). "Consider it all joy, my brethren, when you encounter various trials, knowing that the testing of your faith produces endurance" (James 1:2–3).

Yes, these were very dark days, but I knew He'd sent me to a country that is known for safety, surrounded by the most majestic mountains, the Alps, that are beautifully snow-capped throughout the year. While there I was blessed to travel throughout Europe, bless my sister who only had a year to live with a trip to Europe, her dream, and in the midst of all this, back in the states, my mountain fell with a huge splash!

The courts granted me freedom from all my debt, due to Him causing the courts to actually file a case of bankruptcy on my behalf—something I'd never heard of before or since!

Even though I tried every which way to stop the process, nothing I tried would stop the momentum. Even when I was told I'd have to return to the states to come to the final hearing, and I told them I couldn't—I was so sure the process would stop. It didn't. Instead, I was notified that they were appointing a proxy to stand in on my behalf. Each and every time I tried to stop the process, something outrageously unheard of would happen, keeping the process going.

It wasn't until after I got the final papers in my hand that my Husband told me what I never understood. As He loves to do, He asked me several questions, "Whose debt was this anyway, Michele? Did *you* run up credit card bills? Did *you* spend everything on vacations with another man while *you* were married? Did *you* apply for all those loans that you never intended to pay? Or was all of it someone else's debt?" Tears of relief just flowed down my face as He went on, "You were willing to take the debt, lose everything, your own children, even your country, be humiliated and yet transparent. Now you are free my Love..." and very soon after, I was on a flight back to the states to attend my son's wedding. And believe it or not, God wasn't done.

Even though I indented to return back to Europe to live, I was *given* a home by former neighbors of ours. Yes, given! At first it was discussed to give me the deed, then my Darling spoke to me as I was driving home one evening, saying that taking the house, meant taking on a mortgage, which was far from debt "free." Banks own homes, most people don't. There are a few who do, like a couple of testimonies I shared in this book where God's plan was to buy a home free and clear—and someday that may be His plan for me too. Yet, for now, I love that I am free to move about, without the burden of taxes to pay. Once a door opens for me to live by one of my children or somewhere else entirely—like when I moved to the beach and each of my children came with their families to enjoy the sand and sea--each time I've moved, I never needed to try to find a buyer for my home. Every home on this planet God owns, and as our Husband's bride, He just wants me to live there and enjoy it as my own for as long as I'm there. I've lived where I've paid no rent at all, or at such a reduced rate it shocked people when they found out. Everywhere He's given me favor, sometimes trials (to keep me close to Him as my Husband), but each time where He's had me live has Wowed those who are watching. "You are our letter [an epistle] written in our hearts, known and read by all men" (Corinthians 3:2).

This verse I've known so well for years, "'The silver is Mine and the gold is Mine,' declares the Lord Almighty" (Haggai 2:8). But it took on an entirely new meaning once I was debt free and committed to Him to remain that way no matter what. We all know He owns everything, so why would I or any of His brides choose to be in debt to anyone, not to a bank or mortgage company or credit card company or to drive a car. He has set me free to focus on simply loving others. "Owe no man any thing, but to love one another" (Romans 13:8).

Each time my Husband tells me it's time for us (the two of us, He and I) to go, I just give my notice and off we go, following His lead again and again and again. When something breaks, I notify my landlord whose job it is to get it fixed for me, because He's my Husband and owns it all.

"**The earth is the LORD's**, and all its fullness, the world and those who dwell therein" (Psalms 24:1).

"And he blessed him and said: Blessed be Abram of God Most High, **Possessor** of heaven and **earth**" (Genesis 14:19).

"'The silver is Mine, and the gold is Mine,' says the LORD of hosts" (Haggai 2:8)

"You shall dispossess the inhabitants of the land and dwell in it, for **I have *given* you the land to possess**" (Numbers 33:53).

"Who has preceded Me, that I should pay him? **Everything under heaven is Mine**" (Job 41:11).

"For every beast of the forest is Mine, And the cattle on a thousand hills. I know all the birds of the mountains, And the wild beasts of the field are Mine. "If I were hungry, I would not tell you; **For the world is Mine, and all its fullness"** (Psalms 50:10-12).

"Do you not know that those who minister the holy things eat of the things of the temple, and those who serve at the altar **partake of the offerings of the altar**? Even so the Lord has commanded that those who preach the gospel should live *from* the gospel" (1 Corinthians 9:13-14).

"Now then, if you will indeed obey My voice and keep My covenant, then you shall be My own possession among all the peoples, **for all the earth is Mine**" (Exodus 19:5).

'The land, moreover, shall not be sold permanently, for **the land is Mine**; for you are *but* aliens and sojourners with Me" (Leviticus 25:23).

"Indeed heaven and the highest heavens belong to the LORD your God, also **the earth with all that is in it**" (Deuteronomy 10:14).

Dear bride, if you are still waiting for your Mountain to fall or at least begin to crumble, I hope what I've shared will give you the faith to trust that it will happen at the appointed time.

"Then the LORD answered me and said, 'Record the vision and inscribe it on tablets, that he one who reads it may run. For the vision is yet for the appointed time; it hastens toward the goal and it will not fail. Though it tarries, WAIT for it; for it will certainly come, it will not delay'" (Habakkuk 2:2-3)

It will also happen His way, not yours.

"'For My thoughts are not your thoughts, neither are your ways My ways,' declares the Lord. 'For as the heavens are higher than the earth, so are My ways higher than your ways, and My thoughts than your thoughts'" (Isaiah 55:8–9).

And *when* it happens it will come with the sort of freedom you never imagined could be yours.

"Whom the Son has set free is free indeed" (John 8:36).

Let me close my epilog with my newest favorite verse that should unleash your imagination into what I know He has for you, dear sweet bride.

"Now glory be to God, who by His mighty power at work within us is able to do far more than we would ever dare to ask or even dream of—infinitely beyond our highest prayers, desires, thoughts, or hopes" (Ephesians 3:20 TLB). Dream big!

> "You will say to this mountain,
>
> 'Move from here to there,' and it will move;
>
> And nothing will be impossible to you."
>
> —Matthew 17:20

About the Author

Michele Michaels came to Restore Ministries International when she was facing divorce. At the time she was the mother of two small boys. After reading *How God Can and Will Restore Your Marriage* and *A Wise Woman* and she began helping Erin Thiele with her books, soon after they met while each was in Orlando, Florida. Very soon after Erin visited Michele in her home in Colorado, her marriage was restored.

Almost exactly fourteen years later Michele found herself facing divorce again while helping to update and revise a small Facing Divorce booklet for her church. After returning to RMI to Refresh her mind, Michele began to realize He had planned to use this trial for much good. It was during this new chapter in her life when Michele discovered the real reason God allowed another divorce to happen again and what she had been missing: The Abundant Life.

Michele's book *Moving Mountains* is the fourth book in a series available on **EncouragingBookstore.com** and also on **Amazon.com**.

Also, if you've not read the first three books, make sure you read Michele's book *Finding the Abundant Life, Living the Abundant Life*, and *Poverty Mentality* available from these same booksellers.

Check what is Also Available
on EncouragingBookstore.com & Amazon.com

Scan the code below to the available books for our Abundant Life, Restored and By the Word of Their Testimony series.

Please visit our Websites where you'll also find these books as FREE Courses for both men and women.

Want to know more how you can Live an Abundant Life?

Restore Ministries International
POB 830 Ozark, MO 65721

For more help
Please visit one of our Websites:

EncouragingWomen.org

HopeAtLast.com

LoveAtLast.org

RestoreMinistries.net

RMIEW.com

RMIOU.com

Aidemaritale.com (French)

AjudaMatrimonial.com (Portuguese)

AmoreSenzaFine.com (Italian)

AyudaMatrimonial.com (Spanish)

Eeuwigdurendeliefde-nl.com (Dutch)

EternalLove-jp.com (Japanese)

EvliliginiKurtar.com (Turkish)

Pag-asa.org (Tagalog Filipino)

UiteindelikHoop.com (Afrikaans)

Wiecznamilosc.com (Polish)

ZachranaManzelstva.com (Slovak)

EncouragingMen.org

www.ingramcontent.com/pod-product-compliance
Lightning Source LLC
LaVergne TN
LVHW051054080426
835508LV00019B/1872